101
GREAT
CHOICES
SAN FRANCISCO

101 GREAT CHOICES
SAN FRANCISCO

Anne Bianchi

Printed on recyclable paper

PASSPORT BOOKS
NTC/Contemporary Publishing Company

Library of Congress Cataloging-in-Publication Data

Bianchi, Anne, 1948–.
     101 great choices—San Francisco / Anne Bianchi.
       p.   cm.
     ISBN 0-8442-8989-2
     1. San Francisco (Calif.)—Guidebooks.   I. Title.
    F869.S33B53   1997
    917.94′610453—dc21   97-18693
                                   CIP

Cover and interior design by Nick Panos
Cover and interior illustrations by Chris Horrie
Maps: © 1996 Mapping Specialists, Madison, WI

Copyright © 1997 by NTC/Contemporary Publishing Company
Published by Passport Books
An imprint of NTC/Contemporary Publishing Company
4255 West Touhy Avenue, Lincolnwood (Chicago), Illinois 60646-1975 U.S.A.
Manufactured in the United States of America
International Standard Book Number: 0-8442-8989-2

15   14   13   12   11   10   9   8   7   6   5   4   3   2   1

San Francisco: A Great Choice

I initially came to San Francisco eight years ago during a particularly bad New York winter. My first memory is of driving in from the airport and noticing all the beautiful flowers blooming profusely on the highway's median strip. When I got into town, I went to Russian Hill where I was staying, put down my bags, and went immediately outside. The sun was shining, and there was a clear view of San Francisco Bay. I walked down the street past fragrant flower boxes and perfect little front gardens and stood at the top of the Larkin steps gazing out at that world-renowned body of water speckled with grassy islands. And suddenly I started to cry from the sheer beauty of it all.

I have since been back each winter for three-month stretches, during which I always fall prey to the same phenomenon: being reduced to tears by San Francisco's seemingly infinite beauty. A local writer once said that it's a good thing the early settlers landed on the East Coast; if they'd landed in San Francisco, the rest of the country would still be uninhabited. Ain't it the truth?

It is not only the beauty, however, that continues to draw me here. It's also the people, the lifestyle, the community ethic, the diversity, the sophistication, and the "aw heck, let's try it" attitude. One of my favorite anecdotes concerns the year San Francisco decided there was too much graffiti on the MUNI buses. A notice was posted in the local paper inviting caring residents to come down to the bus yard on a Saturday morning in March with buckets and brushes and spend a few hours cleaning bus interiors.

On a lark, I decided to go, and the event sticks in my mind as a perfect example of why this town functions so well. Hundreds of people showed up—young people, old people, teenagers, and immigrants who could barely speak English. Everybody worked from 9 A.M. until noon, laughing, joking, and talking with people around them as if it were all one big picnic.

One of the things that makes San Francisco such a great place to visit is that its residents think it's such a great place to live. One of the best things to do here is to just walk around gazing at the buildings, houses, parks, views, and people. Wherever you go, wherever you rest your eyes, there will be something wonderful to see, from the hundreds of world-renowned attractions like Golden Gate Bridge, Alcatraz, and "the Crookedest Street in the World" to the little jewels that visitors often overlook, like Ross Alley with its resident Fortune Cookie Factory and noontime concerts at Old St. Mary's Cathedral.

It's a world-class city in every sense, with more drama and civility packed into its 47.4 square miles than any other city on earth. Americans love it because of its original freewheeling reputation. "Things happen first in San Francisco" is a feeling shared by even New Yorkers (although grudgingly). Europeans love it because they feel very much at home in what is clearly the most European of American cities. Hispanics love it because it retains so much of its original Spanish heritage; Asians love it because of its definitive Pacific Rim flavor. Gays and lesbians love it because they feel well represented and welcome; women love it because they can walk around late at night and still feel safe; and families love it because it's a cultural capital with lots of green space and dozens of great tourist attractions geared toward kids. There is something for everybody here and everybody who comes goes away feeling nourished and refreshed.

The City at a Glance

Transportation

Getting to San Francisco "San Francisco has only one drawback," said Rudyard Kipling. "'Tis hard to leave." While that is undoubtedly true, it is very easy to get to. The area is served by two airports: San Francisco International (SFO) and Oakland International (OAK). SFO is 14 miles south of downtown (20–30 minutes); OAK is in the East Bay (30–40 minutes). Most major domestic and international carriers fly in and out of both.

From SFO, you can drive into the city on either Highway 101 or Interstate 280 via Interstate 380. If you're not driving yourself, you can get there via passenger van, taxi, or limousine. Passenger van service delivers you directly to your door; some drivers even carry in your luggage. The Yellow Airport Express (415) 282-7433 and the Supershuttle (415) 871-7800 cost about $10 each and transport no more than three people at a time. Catch them on the upper level of the airport. The SFO Airporter also offers service to all major hotels on Union Square with departures every 15 minutes on the lower level. Fare is $9. For information, call (415) 495-8404.

Taxi service from SFO to downtown costs approximately $24 and can be arranged on the lower level. Volunteer ride sharing for up to three people is allowed; each person pays a share of the tab. For more information about ride sharing (to or from the airport) call (800) SFO-2008 or stop by one of the information booths in the baggage claim area. Limo service can also be arranged at the information booth.

Another option is to take a SamTrans bus, which leaves from the airport's upper level every 30 minutes between 6 A.M. and 12:30 A.M. The bus travels along Mission Street and stops at First, Third, Fifth, Seventh, and Ninth streets.

From OAK, you can either take the shuttles, taxis, or limos, or you can take the Air-BART (Bay Area Rapid Transit) shuttle that drops you off at the Coliseum/Oakland BART station; from there, you can travel by train into the city. The shuttle picks up passengers at Terminals 1 and 2 and at Airport Drive and Armstrong Street. For information, call (510) 839-2882.

You can also take Paramount Limousines (510) 569-5466 or a taxi from one of the following companies: Associated Cabs (510) 893-4991, Yellow Cab (510) 444-1234, or Goodwill (510) 836-1234.

Getting Around San Francisco There's no shortage of ways to get around the city, but probably the best way is walking. A few tips before starting: (1) There is no way to actually avoid the hills, so don't bother. The best you can do is try to minimize the grade—an exercise that puts you squarely in the realm of San Francisco's natives, who all have individual strategies. (2) Always dress in layers—one neighborhood's sunshine is another's fogbelt. Whatever the neighborhood, the city's weather changes from minute to minute, so be prepared with an extra sweater and maybe even an umbrella. (3) Stretching your calves at the end of the day makes it much easier to get going the next morning. No city has hills like San Francisco's, and most people's muscles are just not used to that kind of workout.

For longer stretches, your options include the MUNI buses, the Municipal Railway, the Bay Area Rapid Transit System (BART), taxis, ferries, and, of course, the clanking, groaning, glorious cable cars.

First the buses. If you stay in San Francisco longer than a few days, you will undoubtedly hear residents complaining about the bus system. Generally clean and efficient and sporting a cadre of polite and knowledgeable drivers, they are, nonetheless, an enduring source of dismay to city residents, who constantly clamor for a system-wide revamping, which might even include toll-free ridership.

Despite local dismay, MUNI buses are the fastest way to get around the city. All buses are marked with destinations posted on the front. Stops are marked by pole signs, street markings, or yellow bands on adjacent utility poles. The most frequently used bus stops have plexiglass shelters, where system-wide MUNI maps are posted. Route information is also published in the *Yellow Pages*, or you can call 673-MUNI. MUNI Metro streetcars operate on tracks, which are underground downtown, and above ground in the outer neighborhoods.

Adults pay $1 to ride the MUNI system (excluding cable cars); children and seniors, 35 cents. Free transfers are valid for two changes of vehicle in any direction within two hours, although some drivers (known as "good guys") issue transfers for longer periods of time. If you're going to be doing some concentrated riding, you should definitely consider a MUNI Passport, which offers unlimited travel for one day ($6), three days ($10), or seven days ($15) and is valid on all MUNI regularly scheduled service, including cable cars. Passports are sold at the San Francisco Visitor Information Center on the lower level of Hallidie Plaza (900 Market Street at Powell); the TIX Bay Area, Stockton Street on Union Square; and MUNI, 949 Presidio (near Geary), Room 239.

Cable cars are part of the MUNI system and operate along three routes. The Powell-Hyde line starts at Powell and Market streets and terminates at Victorian Park near the Maritime Museum and Aquatic Park. The Powell-Mason line also begins at Powell and Market but ends at Bay and Taylor near Fisherman's Wharf. The California Street line runs along California from Market Street to Van Ness Avenue. Cable cars cost $2 each way regardless of how old or young you are, and there are no free transfers between lines. If you're planning to do a lot of riding on these wonderful museum pieces, buy either a MUNI Passport or a cable car Day Pass, which costs $6 and allows unlimited travel.

The 71-mile BART system links eight San Francisco stations with Daly City to the south and 25 East Bay stations, including several in Berkeley and Oakland. Trains are clean, safe, and efficient and operate Monday through Friday 4 A.M. to midnight, Saturday 6 A.M. to midnight, and Sunday 8 A.M. to midnight. The fare is 90 cents between all San Francisco train stations and a maximum of $3.45 for travel to the farthest East Bay location. Discount tickets are available for people 65 or older, people with disabilities, and children ages 5 through 12.

BART fare cards can be purchased inside the stations from automated machines and are destination oriented: they will take you only as far as the destination you have paid for. To use a card, place it in a slot on the turnstile, and it will automatically register your point of entry before popping back up. When you exit at the end of your trip, you again place the fare card in a turnstile slot. This time when it pops back up, the fare will have been deducted automatically.

If you want a taxi, you have to call for pickup. Generally, the drivers are prompt and geographically knowledgeable. Taxi fares are approximately $1.70 for the first mile, $1.80 for each additional mile. Three you might try are Veteran's Taxicab Company (415) 552-1300, Yellow Cab (415) 626-2345, and City Cabs (415) 468-7200.

You cannot visit San Francisco without taking a ferry at least once. There are basically three lines to choose from and each goes to a variety of places: The Blue & Gold Fleet at Pier 39 (Fisherman's Wharf) (415) 705-5444, the Red & White Fleet at Piers 41 and 43½ (Fisherman's Wharf) (415) 546-2700, and the Golden Gate ferries at the Ferry Building at the foot of Market Street (415) 923-2000.

For more information, call the San Francisco Visitor's Bureau at (415) 974-6900 or drop by the Visitor's Information Center on the lower level of Hallidie Plaza, 900 Market Street (at Powell). You can also call the Visitor Information Center Hotline to find out everything from who's currently performing in the city's clubs to who's playing baseball at 3Com (formerly Candlestick) Park. Hotline information is available in five languages: English (415) 391-2001, French (415) 391-2003, Spanish (415) 391-2122, Japanese (415) 391-2101, and German (415) 391-2004.

Neighborhoods

"You wouldn't think such a place as San Francisco could exist," wrote poet Dylan Thomas. "The wonderful sunlight there, the hills, the great bridges, the Pacific at your shoes. Beautiful Chinatown. Every race in the world. The sardine fleets sailing out. The little cable cars whizzing down the city hills. . . . And all the people are open and friendly." In other words, it's quite a place. And nowhere are the city's extraordinary qualities more evident than in its neighborhoods—over 20 of them—each buzzing with uniquely diverse ethnic and cultural rhythms. Here are a few to whet your appetite:

Chinatown The entrance gate at Grant and Bush is called the "Dragon's Gate." Inside you'll find 24 city blocks of hustle and bustle where you can buy ancient potions from herb shops, relax and enjoy a dim sum lunch, or witness the making of fortune cookies. It's the largest Chinatown in the United States, and each February it serves as the focal point for the city's most popular festival, Chinese New Year. Chances are that much of what you find in Chinatown, you won't find on Main Street, U.S.A.

North Beach Rich in Italian heritage, North Beach compresses cabarets, cafes, jazz clubs, galleries, inns, family-style restaurants, and gelato parlors into less than a square mile. Bakeries and delicatessens serve up such traditional Italian delicacies as prosciutto, pecorino cheese, mozzarella di bufala, and sacripantina. A perfect spot for an afternoon cappuccino and espresso, North Beach by night is transformed into an exciting playground featuring all types of live music. Don't miss the wonderful mural on the outside wall on the northwest corner of Columbus, Grant, and Broadway: it's a three-paneled microcosm of life in this quirky little enclave.

Fisherman's Wharf One of the city's most vibrant neighborhoods, Fisherman's Wharf was originally home to the fishermen and dock workers who turned early San Francisco into a world-class seaport. Today that same frenetic energy is channeled into a number of points of interest, including Jefferson Street with its clamorous family attractions (Ripley's Believe It or Not, the Wax Museum, the Medieval Dungeon), and three multilevel shopping complexes (the Anchorage, the Cannery, and Ghirardelli Square), all with specialty boutiques, restaurants, and open-air street performance spaces. The wharf is also home to the San Francisco Maritime National Historic Park, whose most famous inhabitants are a colony of boisterous sea lions that have taken up residence at Pier 39 and Pier 41. Other wharf attractions include outdoor vendors selling Dungeness crabs from steaming cauldrons, and Pier 39, the second most visited tourist attraction in California and the home port of the Blue & Gold Fleet, which ferries visitors around the bay.

Union Street The first neighborhood to convert its gingerbread Victorians into popular boutiques, art galleries, and restaurants, Union Street's turn-of-the-century architecture sits in striking contrast to its fashionable modern-day identity. Numerous coffee houses serve some of the best caffe latte in the city, and dozens of bars serve as an irresistible magnet for the singles set. The most famous bar area, the "Bermuda Triangle," is located a block from Union Street at Greenwich and Fillmore. Among Union Street's historic buildings, be sure to visit the Octagon House at 2645 Gough, which was built in 1861, and the 1905 Vedanta Temple at 2963 Webster.

Russian Hill A terrific neighborhood filled with neat houses and tree-lined walkways, Russian Hill's commercial center is Polk Street, with wall-to-wall coffee bars and restaurants of every ethnic variety. Its steep streets, too demanding for automobiles, are often replaced by charming stairways, and its numerous alleyways perpetually confound tourists bent on finding the real-life model for Armistead Maupin's *Tales of the City*. Don't leave without checking out the Real Foods Company on Polk Street between Broadway and Vallejo, a mecca for health-conscious yuppies and trendy food-faddists.

Nob Hill Once the place where railroad magnates rubbed shoulders with rich Gold Rush bankers, Nob Hill's present-day roster of noble tenants include Grace Cathedral, which is a replica of Paris's Notre Dame; Huntington Park, site of numerous art shows and graced by a replica of a 16th-century Roman fountain; a bevy of grand hotels; and dozens of trendy restaurants. Try to structure your Tuesday sightseeing so you have time for the calming noontime classical concerts held at Old St. Mary's Cathedral.

Pacific Heights Stately Victorians crown hills blessed with glorious views of San Francisco's most prestigious neighborhoods and the bay. Consulates, finishing schools, and condominiums share this tree-lined perch with the city's wealthiest families. Jackson Street, near the northwest corner of Alta Plaza Park, is a good place to begin a tour of the neighborhood's mighty mansions. Try the corner of Fillmore and Broadway for an excellent photo shot of the bay and beyond.

Japantown More than 12,000 Japanese-Americans live in this part of Soko or San Francisco. Its focal point is Japan Center, which stretches for three square blocks bounded by Post, Geary, Laguna, and Fillmore. The Center houses shops, restaurants, art galleries, movie theaters, Japanese baths, and a block-long pedestrian mall, with cobbled streets and flowering plum and cherry trees. The best time to visit Japantown is during the spring Cherry Blossom Festival, when the area hums with Japanese music and dance, tea ceremonies, and martial arts and flower arranging demonstrations.

Haight-Ashbury The 1967 "Summer of Love" lives on in this quirky little neighborhood filled with colorfully painted Victorians (along Masonic, Piedmont, and Delmar Streets), vintage clothing, book and record stores, innovative restaurants, and Buena Vista Park, which offers wonderful views of the city. It's fun to take a walking tour of houses once belonging to former residents such as Janis Joplin (112 Lyon Street) and the Grateful Dead (710 Ashbury Street).

The Castro Steep streets and brightly painted Victorians give this Upper Market neighborhood a distinct San Francisco look. The Castro is crammed with imaginative boutiques, bookstores, and bars. The Names Project at 2362 Market Street houses the AIDS memorial quilt. The Castro Theater at 429 Castro survives as the Grand Dame of old-time movie palaces, featuring revivals and prefilm concerts played on the theater's mighty Wurlitzer. Each June, the Gay and Lesbian Freedom Day Parade draws nearly 500,000 participants and spectators.

Golden Gate Three miles long and a half-mile wide, Golden Gate Park is one of the world's greatest urban parks. This green treasure is covered with grassy meadows, wooded trails, secluded lakes, garden groves, several museums, a herd of bison (don't worry, they graze in an enclosed paddock just off Kennedy Drive), and even a beach. Every Sunday from dawn to dusk, strollers, roller bladers, and bicyclists are allowed free run of John F. Kennedy Drive, which closes to traffic. The greater Golden Gate recreational area also encompasses the world's most celebrated bridge, as well as the Presidio, which, until recently, was the oldest continuous military base in the country. Now part of the Golden Gate National Recreation Area, the Presidio contains picnic areas, two beaches, two golf courses, forested hiking trails, and numerous historic sites.

The Mission The heart of San Francisco's predominantly Latino neighborhood is 24th Street, a colorful collection of restaurants, taquerias, Mexican bakeries, produce markets, and specialty shops. Mission Dolores at 16th and Dolores streets is the oldest building in San Francisco. Many of the city's pioneers are buried in the adjacent cemetery. The area also encompasses the largest concentration of murals in the city.

South of Market Also called SOMA, this is the city's hot rock, jazz, and art club neighborhood. Trendy restaurants and dance clubs cram the area, with most of the action taking place on 11th Street between Folsom and Harrison streets. SOMA also encompasses the new Center for the Arts, a $44 million multisite entertainment and art complex comprising Yerba Buena Gardens at 701 Mission Street, the Moscone Convention Center, the San Francisco Museum of Modern Art (SFMOMA) at 3rd and Howard streets, and a variety of other museums and galleries, including the Ansel Adams Center for Photography at 250 Fourth Street and the Cartoon Art Museum at 814 Mission Street.

Weather

Many are the people who come to San Francisco in summer and complain about its "awful weather," by which they mean cold. The problem, as with so many other things in life, is misinformation. San Francisco is not Los Angeles ("Thank God," say the majority of its residents), and, unlike Los Angeles, it never gets really hot. The area is blessed with a temperate marine climate and enjoys mild weather year-round, which is wonderful unless you come here in August expecting to go out at night in shorts.

Here are San Francisco's average high temperatures in degrees Fahrenheit:

January—60°	July—65°
February—60°	August—65°
March—62°	September—69°
April—64°	October—68°
May—65°	November—63°
June—66°	December—55°

Temperatures rarely rise above 75°F or fall below 40. In the summer, however (and this is mainly why tourists complain), the fog rolls in sometimes twice a day—in the early mornings and late afternoons. But it seldom stays long and it's a good idea to view it through the eyes of the locals, who see the fog as just another of San Francisco's gorgeous attractions. Think of all those postcard views of the Golden Gate Bridge rising above a thick, snowy fog bank and you realize how right they are.

For maximum comfort, always be prepared with a light jacket or coat. Imitate local residents who always travel with a what-if bag containing an umbrella and an extra sweater. (Hmmm, that's the reason for all those backpacks!) At night, you will definitely need to wear something warm. Keep in mind that in the summer, lightweight summer clothes can only be worn in the middle of a sunny day.

Banking/Currency

Banks in San Francisco are open 10 A.M.–3:30 P.M. Monday–Thursday and 10–6 on Friday. Most major banks change foreign currency and all types of traveler's checks for face value, although some charge for the privilege. Exchange bureaus that change foreign currency or traveler's checks can also be found at both San Francisco and Oakland airports. Hotels generally will not engage in any form of foreign currency exchange.

Exchange office information is as follows:

American Express 237 Post Street, Monday–Friday 9 A.M.–5 P.M., Saturday 10 A.M.–5 P.M. (415) 981-5533.

Deak International 100 Grant Street near Union Square, Monday–Friday 9 A.M.–5 P.M. (415) 362-3452.

Thomas Cook 425 Market Street, Monday–Friday 9 A.M.–5 P.M. (415) 995-2000.

If you need money wired in a hurry, the quickest way is to have it sent to the nearest Western Union office (800) 325-6000, which charges 10 percent for the service. Its main office is at 697 Howard Street in SOMA (Monday–Friday 7 A.M.–12 A.M.). Thomas Cook provides the same service, but it takes 24 hours and costs approximately $40.

Sightseeing

Organized tours are great ways to experience the city, especially if you have a specialized interest. Here's a few you might want to try. For a more complete list, contact the SFO Visitor's Center (415) 391-2000.

Hornblower Dining Yachts   Have dinner aboard an elegant yacht as you cruise past the sights of San Francisco Bay. You have two choices. The first is a three-hour dinner/dance cruise with a four-course, sit-down dinner and a live band. Cruises leave from Pier 33 at the Embarcadero at 7:30 P.M. Monday through Saturday, or at 6 P.M. on Sunday. Attire is semiformal. The cost is $61.50 per person Sunday through Thursday, $70 per person Friday, and $74.50 on Saturday. The other option is a 2½-hour casual cruise that features an all-you-can-eat buffet, as well as DJ music for dancing, karaoke, and a gaming casino. Leaves at 7:35 P.M. on Friday and Saturday. The price is $54.90 per person. Prices for both tours are exclusive of beverages and gratuities.

Bay Aero Tours   Spectacular one-hour flights over the San Francisco Bay Area. The cost of $55 per person (third person free) includes hotel pickup. Custom photography flights also available. Call (415) 207-0044 or (510) 632-6763.

Gray Line Sightseeing Tours   Offers a variety of ways to see the city. Half-day tours are 3½-hour daily bus trips to most of the city's major attractions, cost $26, and leave at various times. Full-day tours are the same as half-day ones but add on a ferry visit to Alcatraz. The fare is $38 and departure times vary. Around the Bay with Dinner is a four-hour tour leaving at 6 P.M. daily, at $56; and the four-hour tour of Chinatown with dinner for $40 also leaves daily at 6 P.M. All tours depart from Union Square. For more information, call (415) 558-9400.

Wine & Dine Tours   Discover off-the-beaten path Napa Valley wine boutiques on personalized tours led by former Napa chef David Mitchel. Meet and greet winery owners on an eight- to nine-hour tour (pick up and delivery from the Bay Area), which includes lunch and Napa Valley champagne. The cost is $75 per person.

San Francisco Quotables

"Leaving San Francisco is like saying good-bye to an old sweetheart. You want to linger as long as possible."
Walter Cronkite

"If you're alive, you can't be bored in San Francisco. If you're not alive, San Francisco will bring you to life."
William Saroyan

"You know what it is? San Francisco is a golden handcuff with the key thrown away."
John Steinbeck

"Your city is remarkable not only for its beauty. It is also, of all the cities in the U.S., the one whose name conjures up the most visions and more than any other, incites one to dream."
Georges Pompidou, former French president

"It's simply a very romantic place. It's so beautiful and there's that location and the sense of free spirit—who wouldn't become ravenous in such a place?"
Julia Child

"What I like best about San Francisco is San Francisco."
Frank Lloyd Wright

"Of all the cities in the U.S. I have seen, San Francisco is the most beautiful."
Nikita Khrushchev

"I didn't realize until I grew up and went to Los Angeles that we had such a safe and clean city."
Barbara Eden

"Everybody has a favorite city. I have two, London and San Francisco. This fortuitous mating of marine grandeur and terrestrial snugness is what makes the place, to me, the most individual and engaging of American cities."
Alistair Cooke

"When you get tired of walking around in San Francisco, you can always lean against it."
Unknown

Publications/Media

San Francisco has two major newspapers, the *San Francisco Examiner*, which comes out in the afternoon, and the more popular *San Francisco Chronicle*, whose Sunday "Datebook" section (the pages are pink) contains listings of everything that's happening everywhere. Until recently, the *Chronicle* was the home of Herb Caen, a Pulitzer Prize–winning San Francisco institution who wrote an insider column featuring charmingly editorialized snippets about the city's people and events. When Caen died early in 1997, the city virtually came to a standstill.

The *Bay Guardian* is an alternative weekly with definitely left-of-center stories as well as listings of events. The *Bay Area Reporter* is similar to the *Guardian* but is written from a gay perspective. *SF Weekly* lists events in much the same way as the other two and, like them, is free.

Many neighborhoods also have their own paper, which you can pick up in stores and restaurants. Some of the best include *North Beach Now*, *The Marina Times*, and *The Presidio*.

San Francisco Focus is the best of the monthly magazines focused on this miraculous city. Published by KQED, the local public television station, it contains feature stories and events lists. *SOMA* is another San Francisco–centered monthly, albeit much glossier and hipper than the *Focus*.

You can find ethnically focused papers, such as *The Jewish Bulletin* or the local version of the *Irish Echo*, at newsstands that carry a wider range of publications.

Safety/Emergencies

While no one pretends San Francisco is completely safe, you are unlikely to have to deal with crime, which is generally restricted to the most untouristy places. Most of the city's violent crime is drug-related and concentrated outside the region's immediate geographical boundaries. In other words, relax.

If something does happen, however, here are a few phone numbers to have on hand:

Traveler's Aid: (415) 781-6738
Rape Crisis Line: (415) 647-7273
Police/Fire Department/Ambulance: 911
San Francisco Police Department: (415) 553-1373

HOLIDAYS

January 1   New Year's Day
January 15   Martin Luther King's Birthday
Third Monday in February   President's Day
Easter Monday
Last Monday in May   Memorial Day
July 4   Independence Day
First Monday in September   Labor Day
Second Monday in October   Columbus Day
November 11   Veteran's Day
Fourth Thursday in November   Thanksgiving Day
December 25   Christmas Day

FESTIVALS

Chinese New Year   end of January or early February
St. Patrick's Day   March 17
Cherry Blossom Festival   late April
Cinco de Mayo   weekend nearest May 5
Lesbian and Gay Freedom Day   last Sunday in June
4th of July Fireworks
Castro Street Fair   early October
Halloween   October 31

San Francisco Don'ts

Don't wear a bathing suit to North Beach; it's the cafe-studded Italian quarter.

Don't stand directly behind a cable car gripman; you'll get the wind knocked out of you when he jerks back on the brake lever.

Don't pack a tropical wardrobe; the mercury hovers around 60 degrees even in summer.

Don't park on a hill or even a slope without turning your wheels to the curb, setting the hand brake, and putting the car in gear; it's the law.

Don't plan to diet; this is a Weight-Watchers' Waterloo.

Don't send for an ambulance if you hear a chorus of moans, groans, grunts, and wails; it's the foghorns.

Don't pay full price for theater and symphony tickets; try the TKTS booth at Union Square, which sells half-price, day-of-performance tickets.

Don't call cable cars trolleys; they're powered not by electricity, but by cables humming beneath the street.

Don't pop for an imported vintage; you're in the capital of the California wine country.

Don't plan to go swimming in the San Francisco Bay unless you're a member of the Polar Bear Club.

Don't forge past a street sign saying "Grade" or "Hill" unless you've had your brakes checked recently; it means steep, as in 31.5% grade.

Don't board public transportation without exact change; drivers don't make change.

Don't go to Chinatown during Chinese New Year (between mid-January and late-February) if you have delicate eardrums.

Don't be surprised if you're fogged-in one minute and can see forever the next; coastal mists are capricious.

Don't color the bridge over the Golden Gate gold; it's red-orange.

Don't tell a San Franciscan your favorite city is Los Angeles.

Don't even tell a San Franciscan you're from Los Angeles.

Above all, don't call it "Frisco."

How to Use This Book

101 Great Choices: San Francisco is your guide to a sampling of the best the city has to offer in accommodations, dining, parks & gardens, museums & galleries, and other attractions.

Entries are arranged by neighborhoods, from Fisherman's Wharf to Haight-Ashbury to Pacific Heights, and everything in between. Just pick an area you'd like to explore, and this guide will provide you information on interesting things to do and see there. Whether you're interested in sightseeing, dining, shopping, amusing the kids, or enjoying a special entertainment, this handy book will guide you to great choices in any neighborhood.

Attractions are grouped into 11 categories, each identified by a small icon at the top of each entry. If you want to go directly to the best places to eat, shop, take the kids, and so on, use the handy chart below, which list the attractions in this guide by **category** and choice **number.**

Accommodations
12, 20, 21, 33, 39, 44, 48, 60, 62, 80, 83

Children
6, 8, 23, 24, 92

Dining
13, 24, 27, 28, 36, 37, 40, 41, 46, 49, 51, 53, 54, 57, 64, 66, 67, 68, 74, 76, 78, 81, 96

Entertainment & Nightlife
17, 18, 34, 35, 43, 45, 70, 79

Miscellany
7, 31, 38, 47, 61, 63, 75, 85

Museums & Galleries
29, 71, 72, 86, 87, 90

Out of Town
93, 94, 95, 97, 98, 99, 100, 101

Parks & Gardens
3, 4, 65, 88, 91

Shopping
14, 19, 22, 56, 58

Sightseeing
1, 2, 5, 9, 10, 11, 15, 16, 30, 32, 42, 50, 52, 55, 59, 69, 77, 82

Sports & Recreation
25, 26, 73, 84, 89

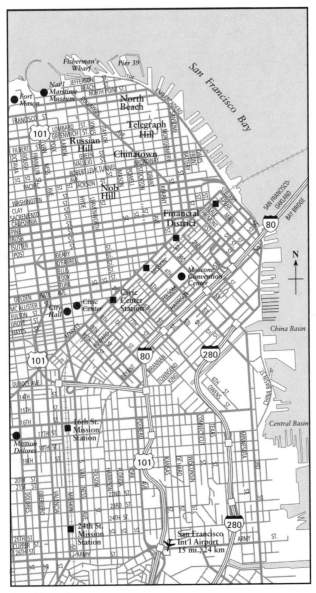

San Francisco

1 / Even in Ruins, a Spellbinder

Alcatraz

Even before you go you realize why it's called *Isla de los Alcatraces*—Isle of the Pelicans. The craggy escarpment rises 135 feet out of the bay, a surprisingly verdant mound of land that looks like a Tuscan hillside village. A once-grim bastion of human suffering, Alcatraz emerged from over a century of isolation on October 26, 1973. On that day, the National Park Service opened it to the public and began running tours from the San Francisco waterfront a mile and a quarter away. The event followed 115 years of federal occupation. The island was used first as a fortification, then as a military prison, army disciplinary barracks, and federal penitentiary. A few of the notorious residents were Al "Scarface" Capone, Robert "The Birdman" Stroud, and the infamous "Three Who Got Away"—Frank Lee Morris and John and Clarence Anglin—who tunneled out in 1962 using sharpened spoons, swam into the bay, and were never heard from again. The last of the Rock's inmates were transferred on March 21, 1963.

Alcatraz is now part of the Golden Gate National Recreation Area, which runs tours of the prison's facilities. These include the main prison block with its steel bars, the claustrophobic (nine-square-foot) cells, the mess hall, the library, visitors' cubicles (including the one used by Mama Capone to talk in Italian to her little darling), and the "dark holes" where recalcitrants languished alone in inky darkness.

But even if you're not into trudging through a dank prison, the trip to Alcatraz is worth it if only for the incomparable views of the skyline and the Golden Gate. You might also be interested in the daily ranger-led programs exploring the island's Native American lore.

The Bay

Alcatraz. Daily ferry service on the Red & White Fleet costs $9 roundtrip, $4.50 for children (both prices include audiocassette rental), and leaves from Pier 41 at Fisherman's Wharf. For information, call (415) 546-2700.

2 / Cruising the Bay

Ferry Rides

With five bridges spanning the waters between San Francisco and its outlying areas, it's hard to believe that ferries were once the only way to cross the bay. But their value as tourist attractions has long replaced—maybe even eclipsed—their worth as a transportation mainstay. The following information will tell you which ferries go where. Remember that it can get very cold out there; dress in layers!

The **Blue & Gold Fleet** offers daily service between Pier 39 at Fisherman's Wharf and Oakland's Jack London Waterfront, where you'll find specialty shops, wonderful restaurants, the legendary author's cabin, and, a short distance away, the USS *Potomac*, FDR's historic pleasure boat. Round trip fare for adults is $7.50 and for children, $3.00; (415) 705-5444. Blue & Gold also offers a 75-minute narrated cruise that travels under both the Golden Gate and Bay bridges and passes pretty close to Alcatraz Island. Fares are $16 for adults and $8 for children; (415) 705-5444.

The **Red & White Fleet** travels daily between Pier 43½ at Fisherman's Wharf and either Sausalito or Tiburon—two dreamy seaport villages where you can stroll around and look at the sights and—if you stay past sunset—get an absolutely priceless view of the San Francisco skyline. Round trip is $11 for adults and $5.50 for children. Red & White also offers one-hour narrated cruises under the Golden Gate Bridge, along the waterfront, through the bay, and past Angel Island and Alcatraz. The fare is $16 for adults and $8 for children; (415) 546-2628.

Golden Gate Ferries on route to Sausalito depart daily from behind the south end of the Ferry Building at the foot of Market Street. Roundtrip fare is $8.50 for adults and $6.40 for children and includes audiocassette rental; (415) 923-2000.

The Bay

3 / An Altogether Heavenly Oasis
Angel Island

If you've been traipsing around town for a few days, you've probably noticed it looming out there and wondered about the person lucky enough to live on such a luxuriously green island in the middle of San Francisco Bay. If it makes you feel any better, only the park rangers live there. Angel Island is a 750-acre state park and an ideal location for picnicking, hiking, or jogging. Two trails lead to the top of 781-foot Mount Livermore—one is an easy hike; the other, moderately hard. Former military structures are located throughout the park; one of them, the Immigration Station at China Cove, is responsible for Angel Island's nickname: Ellis Island of the West.

The island has great traffic-free paths that are perfect for mountain biking; a basic bike can be rented from the central concession for $9/hour or $25/day; $17/hour or $35/day for an expert bike. Tandems are also available at $19/hour or $40/day. For those who prefer to tour by water, there are all-day guided sea kayak trips. The $110 per person fee gets you a picnic lunch, instruction, tour, and all kayaking equipment. Call (415) 488-1000 to make a reservation. You can also take an open-air tram tour of the island for $10 adults and $6 juniors 6–12. Younger children ride free. And if you just can't bear to leave at the end of the day, maybe you can talk your way into one of the nine hike-in campsites available by reservation (you better be a good talker though, because these are usually booked months in advance). To reserve a campsite, call (800) 444-7275.

But if you just want to sit and stare at the spectacular views of the bay, you can do that too—at the Cove Cafe, which features soups, salads, deli-style sandwiches, and the ever-present cappuccino.

The Bay

Angel Island can be reached by ferry, on the Red & White Fleet from Fisherman's Wharf; call (415) 546-2628. Fare is $18. For more information on Angel Island, call (415) 435-1915.

4 / From Swords to Plowshares

The Presidio

For almost 200 years, the Presidio has been an open military post, which also allowed public access to its 1,480 acres of forests and headlands. But in 1989, Congress named it as one of 86 bases to be closed. Since October 1995, when ownership was transferred to the National Park Service, it has become a field of dreams for park service officials, local planners, environmentalists, and visitors from far and near.

While the groundwork is still being laid for civilian use of the Presidio's historic facilities, today's visitors have access to 11 miles of hiking trails, 14 miles of bike routes, and more than 3 miles of beaches.

The number of things to do here boggle the mind. You can fish from a beach or pier within sight of Fort Point, a Civil War brick fortress in the shadow of the Golden Gate. Or you can hike or bike through a redwood forest that was once barren sand dunes. Or golf 18 holes on the second-oldest course in California. Or investigate the Presidio Museum which houses early U.S. military equipment and a cannon left by the Spanish (tours are given on Saturday mornings). Or beachcomb along the bay. Or simply walk along the Presidio coastal bluffs marveling at the views and the sounds of sea lions.

There's also an open area, Crissy Field, which played a major role in early aviation (it's where the first round-the-world flight landed). Closed to planes in 1974, it is now a bay-front recreation area popular with joggers, bicycle riders, windsurfers, beachcombers, and picnickers. *One interesting note*: The (Mikhail) Gorbachev Foundation leases the Presidio's 1890 Coast Guard lifesaving station for its peace-themed think tank.

The Presidio

The Presidio is located along Highway 101, just south of the Golden Gate Bridge and is accessible by MUNI bus lines 43 and 29. The Presidio Golf Course is open daily sunrise to sunset; (415) 561-GOLF.

5 / See the City for $1
Aboard a MUNI Bus
A Ride on the #29

It's a great thing to do on a sunny day when you're tired of walking around and want nothing better than to sit down and experience the city the way locals do. The #29 takes a long circuitous route through the Presidio and Golden Gate Park to Lake Merced and McLaren Park and winds up over by 3Com (Candlestick) Park. You get spectacular views of the bay and Baker Beach as the bus rims the ridge of the Presidio's headlands. Many of the passengers at this point will be people on route to their jobs at the V.A. Medical Center in Lincoln Park.

When you exit the Presidio, you'll travel a bit through the Richmond district before entering Golden Gate Park by Stow Lake and making a long sweep of the Park's south side. You'll exit in the Sunset section and journey the entire length of Sunset Boulevard (no, not that one) until you come to Lake Merced. At this point, the bus will be filled with students on their way to San Francisco State. They'll get off but you'll continue, traveling through the Ingleside and Excelsior sections of the city, eventually arriving at McLaren Park with its wonderful lakes and golf courses. Your journey ends shortly after that at 3Com Park, home of the 49ers and—until they move to their new stadium in the year 2000—the Giants.

At this point, you can either stay on the bus for a return trip or talk to the bus driver about an alternate route back. There's a variety of choices, including a ride on the CalTrain. Whatever you decide, you'll have had a pleasant two-hour trip to places most tourists never see. If you really want to make it special, pack a great lunch and bring some snacks. Bon voyage!

The Presidio

MUNI Bus #29 can be boarded by entering the Presidio at Lombard and Lyon and walking one block to the bus stop. Fare is $1 for adults, 35 cents for children. Exact change is required.

6 / Mental Playground

The Exploratorium

The Exploratorium is to San Francisco what Disneyland is to Anaheim—a great amusement center that feeds every one of the senses. Blow a bubble bigger than a dog. Freeze water with a vacuum. Bend light to make images and rainbows. Move a 400-pound pendulum with a tiny magnet. Listen to a hollow pipe sing.

Some people call it a mad scientist's playpen. Other's say it's the wildest art show in town. Whatever you think as you walk through this moderately noisy, slightly chaotic place, your kids are going to love it. Housed in a cavernous hangarlike building near Golden Gate Bridge, the Exploratorium houses over 700 hands-on exhibits, ranging from an echo tube and a miniature tornado to an antigravity mirror and a table for dissecting cow's eyes.

The museum is the brainchild of the late Frank Oppenheimer, who was its director from 1969 until his death in 1985. Departing from the style of all the museums he had known and disliked for what he called "their inability to engage the thinking process," Oppenheimer designed toylike exhibits that appealed to curiosity and intellect as well as eye and emotion.

Museum "explainers" are on hand to—what else—explain what's going on if you ask. But chances are, your kids are going to get into the spirit of figuring it out for themselves as soon as they walk in the door, which is what this museum is all about.

Don't miss the Tactile Dome, a pitch-black, crawl-through cave where the object is to feel different textures. It's a cross between a maze and a funhouse and is like nothing else you've ever experienced.

The Marina

The Exploratorium, 3601 Lyon Street; (415) 561-0360. Adults $9, youth (6–17) $5, children (3–5) $2.50. Tactile Dome admission is an extra $3.

7 / Songs from the Sea

The Wave Organ

What would the waves say if they could talk? The answer is revealed on the Marina's breakwater, where stonemasons George Gonzalez and Tomas Lipps created a "wave organ" using both recycled granite from old street blocks and headstones recovered from four ancient cemeteries. The project was sponsored by the Exploratorium's artist-in-residence program and creates natural "music" made by waves as they funnel through pipes that run from the breakwater into the bay—it coos, dips, gurgles, swooshes, and hums.

The Wave Organ consists of three granite "listening posts." When the tide is high, say five feet or more, the topmost station issues the soothing baritone sound of the water as it rolls against the shore. As the tide goes out, you can go to the next lower terrace to hear a more high-pitched sound, then even lower for ebb tide, which provides the highest pitch of all.

According to George Gonzalez, the Wave Organ works because pipes going into the stone chambers beneath the water act like compressors to produce the harmonic sounds.

To get to the Wave Organ, walk to the end of Lyon Street around the waterside of the yacht harbor. Along the way, you'll pass the St. Francis and the Golden Gate Yacht clubs. Keep walking until you come to the end of the promontory. The Wave Organ is behind the fenced area and right beyond the sign that says "Keep Out" (addressed to cars, not walkers). The tides must be right to do the Wave Organ justice, but if you've come at the wrong time, take heart and feast on the 360-degree view.

The Marina

8 / Flying High

Kite Flying at Marina Green

Maybe you've flown kites before. Or maybe the idea has always appealed to you, but you've just never gotten around to it. If so, rush down to the Marina Green and surrender yourself to the kite-flying mania that pervades this place on any Sunday with even a hint of sunshine. If you don't make a habit of packing a kite when you travel, make a quick stop at either The Kite Shop at Ghirardelli Square, 900 North Point (415) 673-4559, or Kite Flite at Pier 39 (415) 956-3181. Buy a basic model or splurge and get one of those multilevel box kites favored by so many San Franciscans. Or if you feel like an advanced kite-flyer, buy a fighting kite, which you maneuver by using two separate handles and strings.

But even if you decide against actually participating, go and watch. The Marina Green is a big grassy field-playground on the edge of the bay which offers stunning views of the Golden Gate Bridge and the bay; this is the best spot to watch the hordes of sailboats plying the bay on any given weekend. It's a haven for joggers, in-line skaters, and sunbathers, as well as kite-flyers. Just don't think of chatting up any of the actual flyers—kites are serious business here. More often than not any kids accompanying the kite-flying adults have long given up trying to have their turn and are sitting over on the side playing with something else.

The Marina

Marina Green is on Marina Boulevard between Baker and Buchanan streets.

9 / A Good Place to Sit and Ponder the Imponderable

The Palace of Fine Arts

The 1915 Panama-Pacific International Exhibition left behind many wonderful memories. It also propelled San Francisco into the category of world-class cities. And it contributed one amazing structure—a buff-colored granite dome atop a semicircle fronted by handsome colonnades and embellished with dozens of maidens, many of whom only show us their backs. Like everything else in the exhibition, the structure was scheduled for demolition. But that was before the protestations registered by philanthropist Walter Johnson and hundreds of local citizens. Many years later, the giant dome was again threatened, this time by natural disintegration. Again, the people spoke, and today the Palace of Fine Arts stands majestically next to a tree-shaded lagoon hosting flocks of ducks with an occasional swan or two.

It's a great place to come for a stroll—especially if you combine it with a trip to the Exploratorium (see page 6). You can walk in and around the columns of this Beaux Arts beauty and even experiment with echoes by belting out a song under the central rotunda. At night, the palace is transformed into a lovers' oasis by the son et lumière lights focused on the giant neoclassical structure. Weekends almost always bring a wedding party posed on the grassy lawns against the palace's stunning pink columns. Bring a picnic lunch or retreat afterward to one of Chestnut Street's charming sidewalk bistros.

The Marina

The Palace of Fine Arts, Baker Street off Marina Boulevard.

10 / Have Your Picture Taken Next to an Environmental Hero

Philip Burton Statue

Fittingly, he was placed in the middle of a vast green oasis, where he can look out over his handiwork and feel satisfied that he nudged and prodded on behalf of park preservation. The "he" in question is Philip Burton, head of San Francisco's last political dynasty (both his wife and brother are members of Congress), and a fervent environmentalist who was responsible for preserving much of the city's green space (this one included). His greatest achievement was in writing a law stipulating that if the Army ever left the Presidio, that sprawling landmass would be turned over to the Department of the Interior—a set of circumstances that incredibly came to pass in 1995.

He is sculpted in bronze, a much larger-than-life version of his already towering self, and set in an interesting brick-paved rotunda surrounded by rolling green hills. The statue alone is worth a visit, but when you're done, take a look at the rest of Fort Mason Center. Besides the wonderful parkland surrounding you, there is a lower level (stairway on the east side of the park) containing theaters, galleries, museums (the African American Historical and Cultural Society and the Museo Italo-Americano are located in Building C), and restaurants (notably Greens—the city's best vegetarian restaurant, with a superlative view of the bay).

Fort Mason dates back to the 1800s, when it served as a command post for the army sent to subdue the West. Completed by WPA workers in the 1930s, it is now part of the Golden Gate National Recreation Area, a great place to view the bay and the Golden Gate Bridge if looking north, and Pacific Heights if facing south.

The Marina

Philip Burton Statue is in Fort Mason Center, Marina Boulevard (entrance at Buchanan Street).

11 / Eternally Youthful
San Francisco's Victorian Houses

Ponce de León missed the boat when he didn't journey on to San Francisco. Eternal youth is the rule here, and nowhere is there a better example than the city's oldest dwellings, which get more beautiful with every passing day.

A great part of San Francisco was built between 1850 and 1900, when Victorian architecture was in flower. Some 14,000 residential examples remain, about half of which have been recently restored—an astonishing survival statistic when you consider the mammoth fires that swept the city following the 1906 earthquake. With minor exceptions the fire wiped out the town's entire northeast side. Thus the richest reliquary of Victoriana is west of Van Ness, although the Mission District south of Market Street also has its share.

There are three basic designs: Italianate, characterized by tall, narrow windows and doors and heavy-bracketed roof cornices; Queen Anne, marked by rounded corners, hooded domes, stained-glass windows, and shingles used as siding; and Stick, or Eastlake, with rectangular bay windows, horseshoe arches, and vertical or horizontal "sticks"—wood siding.

Two Victorians are open for tours: The gorgeous 1861 Octagon House at Gough and Union Streets is open to the public three days a month. Call (415) 441-7512 for information. The Haas-Lilienthal House at 2007 Franklin, which is an 1886 Queen Anne, is maintained as a headquarters for the Foundation for San Francisco's Architectural Heritage. Call (415) 441-3004 for tour information.

The greatest concentration of privately owned houses are in the Pacific Heights-Cow Hollow vicinity. Best areas for viewing are: Union, Green, Vallejo, and Broadway between Steiner and Gough; Bush between Divisadero and Laguna; the streets bordering Alta Plaza Park (Scott and Clay); the streets bordering Lafayette Park (Buchanan and Sacramento); and the streets bordering Alamo Park (Steiner and McAllister).

Union Street

12 / When Only the Best Will Do

Sherman House

There are times when it's OK to be practical, and then there are times when nothing short of an all-out splurge will do. A stay at Sherman House fits handily into the latter category. Once the home of Leander Sherman, a wealthy businessman and well-known arts philanthropist, this French-Italianate-style mansion is today a small luxury hotel with eight rooms and six one-bedroom suites. But, oh, what accommodations! Each features a full- or half-canopy queen-sized feather bed, embroidered antique linens, and a wood-burning fireplace. Some offer views of the bay and Golden Gate Bridge, while others overlook the English-style formal gardens that surround the house.

All the main house rooms contain magnificent antique furniture and decorative extras, ranging from window couches, separate English sitting rooms, Biedermeier desks, upholstered walls, to oversized Roman-style tubs. But if you're hankering to really splurge, accept nothing less than a suite in the Carriage House. With free-standing fireplaces, Chinese slate floors, French-paned windows, and private sunken living rooms filled with beautiful French period furnishings, this is definitely what you had in mind when you threw economy to the winds.

While you're at it, you might as well spring for the heavenly California-French cuisine served in the Sherman House Dining Room. The menus are personalized, so you can have any message your little heart desires printed and ready to greet you at the end of a long, hard day of sightseeing.

Union Street

Sherman House, 2160 Green Street. Call (415) 563-3600 or (800) 424-5777. Accommodations from $295 to $825.

13 / An Asian Beer House That Serves Phenomenal Food

Betelnut

Betelnut is styled after Asian beer houses called *pejiu wu*, which serve their own draft beer in large mugs alongside plates of highly seasoned and very spicy local fare known as "street food." The name comes from the betelnut chewed by natives of Southeast Asia as an alternative to caffeine. Chewing betelnut reputedly gives an exhilarating lift and creates mysterious and exotically cleansing flavors.

Betelnut's influences are drawn from all over Asia and are reflected in the highly eclectic menus: there's China ("little dragon" dumplings of pork and shrimp with ginger vinegar), Thailand (spicy coconut chicken with eggplant, lemon grass, and basil), Singapore (gooey, sweet chile crab), and Vietnam (spicy egg noodles with braised beef and spinach), among others.

You can't go wrong whatever you order because it's all phenomenal. You choose from a list containing small plates, large plates, noodles and dumplings, breads and rice, and vegetable sides. Four beers are available on draft; all are created especially for Betelnut by the Golden Pacific Brewery in Mendocino. There's also an unusual collection of eight bottled Asian beers as well as a complete selection of wines.

The restaurant itself is as dramatic and exciting as the food. The 145 seats are scattered over four areas created to resemble an authentic Asian beer house. Walls and ceilings are made from two-inch-wide planks of redwood, and a row of banquettes and tables is set directly opposite the open and very busy kitchen. Make reservations. This is one of the city's most popular moderately priced restaurants (entrées around $13), and it is always very crowded, very noisy, and extremely satisfying.

Union Street

Betelnut, 2030 Union Street (near Buchanan); (415) 929-8855. Open Sunday–Thursday 11:30 A.M.–11 P.M. and Friday–Saturday 11:30 A.M.–midnight.

14 / Shopping Malls, San Francisco Style

Union, Chestnut, and 16th Streets

One of the best ways to get a feel for San Francisco's neighborhoods is to stroll along its shopping streets, taking in the unique store windows and stopping occasionally for a caffe latte.

Start your journey on Union Street where gingerbread Victorians were among the city's first to be converted to tony boutiques, art galleries, and restaurants. Definitely upscale in both appearance and clientele, Union Street's shops sell a variety of things including rice paper lamps, stunning cityscape photographs, the latest in European fashions, and old-world decorative toys. When you're ready to take a break from shopping, pull up a chair at Bepple's Pies and order a slice from the irresistible assortment displayed in the sunny bay window. Union Street's shopping district runs from Fillmore to Gough.

Chestnut Street is similarly upscale although minus the Victorians and plus a few hundred people—especially on weekends. Go on a sunny Saturday when it seems like every neighborhood resident between the ages of 22 and 38 is hanging out somewhere on "The Strip" (between Fillmore and Divisadero). They're either shopping in one of the dozens of distinctive boutiques, eating at one of the numerous small bistros, or simply sitting on the curb slurping a smoothie and tightening the bindings on their rollerblades.

You get a slightly different feel walking along 16th Street between Valencia and Dolores. No less crowded with either unique shops or unusual eateries, this area is characterized by the sort of hipness that includes nose rings and retches at the thought of being called "yuppie." Don't miss La Estrella's baked goods and Bombay Bazaar's collection of Indian spices (on Valencia between 16th and 17th).

Union Street

15 / It Rolls in on Little Cat Feet

Viewing the Fog

When Los Angeles is hot, San Francisco is not. Or ever. If the mercury rises above 75, the locals complain of a heat wave, and if it stays there for more than two days, they peer feverishly seaward. And sure enough, there it comes, trumpeted by a flourish of foghorns!

San Franciscans love their fog—for its beauty as well as for its value as natural air conditioning. For visitors, however, it can be somewhat disconcerting. But only if you overlook the mystical and magical way with that it rolls into the bay, pushing its way above the Golden Gate, drifting and swirling up and over the Marin headlands, and nestling up against shoreline piers.

The following is a list of the best places for fog viewing. Remember: timing is essential. By midday the sun has burned off most of the white wispy stuff, and San Franciscans are shedding their jackets and sweaters to bask in the sun before the fog rolls in again in the late afternoon.

For a heavenly view, rise above the mist atop a San Francisco hill: Broadway in Pacific Heights or one of the streets in Russian Hill is perfect. Look down on the shroud of fog as it enters the Golden Gate, spreading over the bay. Twin Peaks and the top of Coit Tower are also wonderful spots, as is the summit of Mt. Tamalpais, which is just 15 minutes north of the Golden Gate Bridge.

One of the best spots for viewing from afar lies just below the northern end of the Golden Gate Bridge at Vista Point. Known as East Fort Baker, this secluded recreation area affords gorgeous views of the fogged-in bay. Cargo ships, tankers, luxury liners, yachts, and sailboats pass at eye level, greeted by blasts from a traditional foghorn from the Golden Gate Bridge.

Pacific Heights

16 / Lives of the Rich and Famous

The Mansions of Pacific Heights

The Seacliff area of the city has bigger, more ostentatious mansions, but you can't see very many of them because most are hidden behind towering walls or thick hedges. Lofty Pacific Heights however, lets its opulence just hang out in the open for anyone to see, anytime. It's a good place to let your "what if" fantasies run wild.

The best are located on Vallejo, Broadway, and Pacific close to the Presidio. They're all big, all beautiful, and all different. They're also protected geographically from noisy through traffic, which gives them a welcome air of calm and serenity (quiet being one of the many things money can buy).

Jump-start your tour on Broadway and Baker at the top of the Baker steps. Stand for a moment gazing at this particularly patrician view of the bay. The building at 2898 Broadway was designed in 1899 by Walter Danforth Bliss who was also the architect of the St. Francis Hotel and the Metropolitan and University clubs. Next door was once the residence of Ann Getty (yes, of those Gettys). The house on the southeast corner was built by Joseph Strauss, the structural engineer of the Golden Gate Bridge.

The palace at 2850 Broadway was the subject of some controversy when it first appeared in all its aluminum splendor. Things have since calmed down. Continue walking east on Broadway until you come to Normandie Court and the charming set of stone steps at the end of the street. Either take the steps down to Green or continue meandering along Broadway. The wonderful part of this tour is that you can't go wrong— beautiful houses are everywhere! Try to schedule your visit on a sunny day when all the front-garden flowers are open.

Pacific Heights

17 / Blues Through the Night

Rasselas/Biscuits 'n' Blues

When it opened in 1985, the critics expressed their "supreme regret" that Rasselas probably wouldn't last. The music was great, they said, and so was the food. But who would come all the way out to Pacific Heights to hear music? And besides, who even knew what Ethiopian food was? Fortunately, they were wrong. Agnofer Sheferaw, Rasselas's owner, is still here, packing them in seven nights a week. East Bay blues bands are the rule in this small square room which features great acoustics and an adjoining Ethiopian restaurant. The jivin' starts at 9 and if you're not here by then, forget about it. The place is packed! Cover charges range from $3 to $10 with a two-drink minimum. The music venues change nightly.

Biscuits 'n' Blues bills itself as the "Home of the Hot and Fresh Buttery Biscuits That Melt in Your Mouth." Take them at their word. It's a great place to eat soul food and listen to music that comes from the soul. The fried chicken is to die for! The music is no slacker either—all kinds of music (Texas blues, blues/rock, gospel) performed to very appreciative crowds who tend to get emotionally involved. Sundays is "Fried Chicken and Gospel" night, with performances by the up-and-coming Gospel Hummingbirds ($15). Come for dinner and a show, or just for the show. The downstairs space can be smoky and claustrophobic, but you won't be sorry once the music starts. Food prices are moderate, and cover charges range from $5 to $10.

Pacific Heights

Rasselas, 2801 California Street (at Divisadero); (415) 567-5010.

Biscuits 'n' Blues, 401 Mason (at Geary); (415) 292-BLUE.

18 / The Beat Goes On

The Fillmore

San Francisco's early rock venues each have their own rock 'n' roll claim to fame. There's The Warfield, the Winterland Auditorium, the Savoy-Tivoli, Mother's, the Stone, and Wolfgang's. Yet it's the Fillmore Auditorium, one of the birthplaces of modern rock, that bridges the old and the new. Bill Graham called it his "first love," his "mistress." He put on his first show there in 1965. For the next 2½ years it was a mecca for the '60s counterculture. Janis, Jimmie, the Who—they all at one time or another graced the auditorium's dark, dank stage. It was Graham who first introduced audiences to the increasingly diverse musical styles that characterized the era, and it was Graham who first combined black acts like Chuck Berry and B. B. King with white rock groups.

After the 1989 earthquake, the Fillmore found itself in serious need of retrofitting and was forced to close its doors. But Bill Graham always dreamed he would one day return the auditorium to its glory days. Though he died in a helicopter crash in 1991, his dream was carried out by the staff of Bill Graham Presents, which reopened the Fillmore on January 18, 1994, to cheering hordes of rock fans. While the bands that perform there today tend toward a more modern-day rock, there are plenty of reminders of years gone by. The walls are still lined with the psychedelic posters that made the Fillmore famous and—just like in the early days—there's no sign out front advertising its existence, only a burgundy awning.

The Fillmore presents live rock Tuesday through Saturday. There is very limited main floor seating and most people stand. Advance tickets are available with no service charge every Sunday 10 A.M.–4 P.M. at the Fillmore Box Office. Prices vary. Otherwise, you can get tickets at any BASS ticket outlet.

The Fillmore

The Fillmore, 1805 Geary at Fillmore; (415) 346-6000. Shows Tuesday through Saturday, doors open at 8, show at 9.

19 / Venerable Elegance
Fillmore Street's Vintage Clothing Shops

San Francisco is loaded with secondhand clothing stores—some catering to those who simply want to avoid paying new-clothes prices, others specializing in high-end design at low-end prices. The following three options are all located within a few blocks of each other on Fillmore Street in Pacific Heights.

Repeat Performances has a vast clientele of celebrity donors who tend to wear their Armanis once and then drop them off here. After two months in stock, unsold clothing is marked down to half price; after that, it's shipped off to the Salvation Army. If you're lucky, you may just find that Versace you've been ogling in a downtown window for fifty times the price.

Seconds to Go is somewhat different from the other two in its level of organization. The motto here is "Seek and Ye Shall Find." Clothing is scattered in random fashion throughout the store, and there's a good chance of finding something special, if you look hard enough!

The Fillmore

Repeat Performances, 2233 Fillmore; (415) 563-3123. Hours: Monday, Wednesday, Thursday, and Saturday 10 A.M.–4 P.M. Tuesday and Friday, 10 A.M.–6:30 P.M. Major credit cards accepted.

Seconds to Go, 2252 Fillmore; (415) 563-7806. Hours: Monday 10 A.M.–4 P.M., Tuesday through Saturday 10 A.M.–5 P.M. Cash only.

20 / Staying in a French Chateau

The Archbishop's Mansion

In 1904, after completing work on the Great Cathedral of St. Mary's, San Francisco's Archbishop Patrick Riordan decided he also needed a home. The "Mansion," as it came to be known, was occupied by a succession of church hierarchy until 1945 when it fell into disuse. Jonathon Shannon and Jeffrey Ross bought the structure in 1980 and spent the next two years restoring this Belle Epoque French chateau.

Today, the Mansion operates as an inn, with 15 rooms, each custom decorated and including exquisite French antiques, embroidered linens, marble fireplaces, and tapestry-upholstered divans. The period's love affair with opera is reflected in the names of the rooms: Rosenkavalier, Manon, Aida, Daughter of the Regiment, Gypsy Baron, and Italian Girl in Algiers are only a few. The most luxurious is the Don Giovanni Suite, with a grand parlor, two fireplaces, a carved four-poster bed that comes from a French castle, and magnificent views.

From 5:30 P.M. to 7:30 P.M. each evening, guests are treated to a selection of fine wines, which are served in the parlor and complimented by piano selections played on a 1904 Bechstein Grand piano that once belonged to Noel Coward. Breakfast is served in bed, whenever you want it. Nice, huh?

Rates run from $129 to $385 for the Don Giovanni Suite. The Mansion is located on beautiful Alamo Square, between the Financial District and Golden Gate Park. Although it's slightly out of the hotel district, the square is one of the most beautiful settings of the city. Note: Smoking is allowed in the dining room only.

The Fillmore

The Archbishop's Mansion, 1000 Fulton Street; (415) 563-7872.

21 / Traditional Japanese Accommodations

The Radisson Miyako Hotel

The Radisson Miyako Hotel, like San Francisco, is a unique multicultural experience. Its 218 guest rooms and 16 specialty suites are equally divided between Western-style accommodations and traditional Japanese rooms, featuring soft tatami floor mats, raised sleeping platforms with plush futons, shoji screens that open to reveal beautiful rock gardens, redwood saunas, and furos—deep-tub Japanese baths stocked with jasmine-scented bath salts. The hotel provides both Eastern and Western room service as well as a variety of relaxation-oriented services. I heartily recommend the in-room shiatsu (finger-pressure massage). Also, make sure you leave time to wander through the public rooms to view the hotel's $6-million collection of Japanese antique art.

The Miyako is favored by businesspeople drawn to its "Club Room" options, which combine the comfort of Western-style king-sized beds, luxurious marble bathrooms, and oversized whirlpool tubs with business must-haves like double-line phones, voice mail, and fax and computer jacks. But travelers also like to stay here to experience the serene comfort of traditional Japanese accommodations.

The Miyako is located in Japantown at the southern end of Pacific Heights, around the corner from Fillmore Street. It is also one block away from the Japan Center, which contains art galleries, boutiques, Asian restaurants, an eight-theater movie complex, and the celebrated Kabuki Hot Springs, providing traditional Japanese massage and bath treatments.

Japantown

The Radisson Miyako Hotel, 1625 Post Street. Call (415) 922-3200 or fax (415) 921-0417. Rooms range from $109 to $199 and $299 for suites.

22 / When You Have an Uncontrollable Hankering for Chocolate

Ghirardelli Square

Although it's name is synonymous with the converted chocolate factory that sits squarely in its center, Ghirardelli Square is about more than just placating a sweet tooth. It's actually an entire minineighborhood of multilevel shops, open-air public spaces, and breathtakingly beautiful waterfront vistas. But, yes, you can also buy a mega chunk of creamy dark fudge.

Before you give in, however, note the huge red brick building that forms the Square's nucleus. Built in 1900, the Ghirardelli Chocolate Company at one point employed over 2,000 people. The enormous sign on the front of the building was constructed in 1915 and was one of the world's largest electrified signs. During World War II, it was shut down for security reasons.

Ghirardelli Square contains numerous restaurants, bistros, and shops, among them Ann Taylor, The Nature Company, Teaz on the Square (offering 78 varieties of aromatic tea), and the Sharper Image, where you can actually try out various massage machines. When you're done shopping and noshing, head for the luxuriously landscaped waterfront park located at the foot of the Square. With some of the most beautiful bay views in all of San Francisco, the park is regularly visited by Frisbee players, picnickers, and those who just want to catch a few rays of sun. It's a great place to refuel.

Ghirardelli Square

Ghirardelli Square is located next to Fisherman's Wharf at the foot of the Hyde Street Pier.

23 / Local Barkers

Sea Lion Colony

For reasons that nobody has been able to discern, a huge sea lion colony took up residence in the waters between Piers 39 and Pier 41 in January 1990, and the playful pinnipeds have delighted onlookers of all ages ever since. Exhibitionists to their very core, the sea lions never seem to tire of adoring stares from their admirers; they bark, they flip, they race away from the piers and then race back, doing flip turns against the wood docking. Most of all, they lie in the sun, preening for their grateful audience and lustfully exhibiting their sleek chocolate coats. The dozen or so platforms on which they reside were built especially for them a few years ago, when it became clear they had come to stay.

You can view the sea lions any time, day or night, although they seem to have an extra oomph of flair on bright sunny days. Just walk to the end of either pier, following the signs announcing their presence. You'll hear them well before you see them, so don't worry too much about whether you're going in the right direction. Best view is from the upstairs level of Pier 39, right outside the Bay View Cafe (you might want to have lunch at the cafe at one of the windows with a direct view of the sea lions). Free guided tours conducted by docents from Marin County's Marine Mammal Center are offered on weekends from 11 A.M. to 5 P.M.

Fisherman's Wharf

The Sea Lion Colony is on view at the ends of Piers 39 and 41 in Fisherman's Wharf.

24 / It's for People, Not for Boats

Pier 39

Call it a recycled industrial wharf; call it a trendy latter day Playland; call it a kaleidoscope of cute shops all competing for your cash. Whatever you call it, you should know that San Francisco's children consistently point to Pier 39 as the place where they have the most fun. Credit goes to the antique Venetian carousel; the electronic bumper cars; the newly opened 707,000-gallon aquarium roundabout; Music Tracks, where you can record your own song; Dino Island, the adventure ride that is San Francisco's answer to Jurassic Park; the San Francisco Experience, a multimedia movie; and a host of other games, roving food vendors, and penny arcades that cram this 45-acre, boot-shaped pier.

Pier 39's two levels each contain long zig-zaggy boardwalks that wind their way in and around the uneven edge of the bay. There's also a million-dollar view of the bay in all its splendor—bridges, boats, highlands, islands, feathery cloud formations, frothy whitecaps, dappled sunlight, and the occasional puff of fog. Look inland and there's another great view, this time of sophisticated skyscrapers posed against a backdrop of undulating hills.

From here you can catch the Blue and Gold Fleet for a scenic bay cruise, or hop a seaplane for a 30-minute aerial tour. Don't leave without checking out Cybermind's variety of interactive virtual reality games or the Crystal Geyser Center Stage, where San Francisco's best street performers vie for your attention. *Fisherman's Wharf*

Pier 39, on the waterfront between Fisherman's Wharf and the Embarcadero; (415) 981-PIER. Shops open daily 10:30 A.M.–8:30 P.M. Extended summer hours. Restaurants open at 11:30 A.M. The Pier 39 Parking Garage is located directly across the street from Pier 39.

25 / Sausalito Here I Come
Biking the Scenic Bay Trail

Time to try out a new set of muscles—your bike-riding extensors. One of the best bike rides ever starts at Fisherman's Wharf and follows the waterfront along Aquatic Park, through Fort Mason and the Marina District (with incredible views), along Crissy Field to Fort Point (the only Civil War fort west of the Mississippi), and across the Golden Gate Bridge to Sausalito, where you can finally make up for all those burned-off calories by feasting at one of the many waterfront seafood restaurants (try Scoma's).

When you've regained some momentum, park your bike and explore Sausalito's incredibly charming main street with its dozens of boutiques and great views of San Francisco Bay. Once a stomping grounds for artists and misfits, the town is now a mecca for the chardonnay-and-yachting-club set who may live in anything from a $2-million, cedar-shingled bungalow to a houseboat parked in one of the marina alleys along the waterfront. If you feel really adventurous, head up into the hills behind the shopping district to view the village's constantly evolving architecture—San Francisco Victorian meets Marin County Mellow.

And if you feel like lolling at an outdoor cafe with a margarita or two, don't worry. You're not driving home. One of this bike journey's best features is the return trip via ferry. Plan it so you hit the ferry after sunset when the electrified skyline is at its high-voltage best.

A good place to rent bikes is Blazing Saddles, 1095 Columbus Avenue (415) 202-8888. The shop, which carries maps, locks, helmets, water bottles, and anything else you need to make this a truly great experience, is open daily from 9 A.M. to 5 P.M. Rental prices vary according to the type of bike you use. You can keep the bikes overnight at no extra charge in case you are overly seduced by the romantic view and miss the last ferry.

Fisherman's Wharf

26 / The High Priestess of Wackiness
San Francisco Examiner's Bay-to-Breakers Race

In a city known throughout the world for its wacky spectacles, this one takes the cake. Imagine a hundred thousand-plus runners thundering through the streets dressed in all manner of outrageous outfits. Imagine a good number of them tethered together and running in syncopation. You can't, right? All the more reason not to miss the annual Bay-to-Breakers Race held each year in mid-May. This event is so outrageous that it's worth planning your trip around it. Hordes of visitors do—but before going any further, it's important to state that hotels and restaurants overflow during this period. *Translation*: book early. But do book, if only to see the craziness and the costumes firsthand. Past participants have run the race dressed as eggplants, Coit Tower, Roman centurions, and Mae West. Some have even run it undressed. The "centipedes" are everyone's favorites—4 to 40 contestants tied together and running as a unit. There have been centipedes dressed as a horde of killer bees, a contingent of waiters (bearing trays laden with food), a gaggle of nuns, briefcased executives—you name it. There are also, truth be told, about 500 elite runners who compete seriously. But who cares about them? The race begins at 8:00 A.M. and continues until most of the runners have completed the 7½ miles starting from the bay and ending at Ocean Beach, hence the name. Spectators line the route most of the way, and the city pulses with activities both pre and post, including the manic "Footstock Festival" held in Golden Gate Park's Polo Field.

Waterfront

San Francisco Examiner's **Bay-to-Breakers Race**. For information, call (415) 777-7773. Race Hotline: (415) 512-5000 x222. Race entry fee: $14. Held in mid-May.

27 / Comfort Food and Russian Hill Charm

Sinclair's Le Petit Cafe

If your image of a quaint San Francisco bistro revolves around wood floors, bent wood chairs, dark pine wainscoting, and a yuppie clientele that sometimes looks like a "Friends" tryout, this is the place for you. Originally called Le Petit Cafe, this shoebox-size gathering place is neatly woven into a neighborhood of tree-lined streets and more coffee bars than you'd find in all of South Dakota. Owner Mark Sinclair's résumé includes a series of uppity locales like Seasons in Boston and the French Room in San Francisco's Clift Hotel. But he obviously—and consciously—ditched his pretensions in creating this homey, intimate place with what he calls "comfort food" and service so personal that you're often served by Mark himself.

The most expensive main course is less than $10, and it's an amazing value considering the quality and quantity. Sinclair chooses the wines and beers himself; his list is varied, imaginative, and reasonably priced.

But dinners are not the only notable thing about this place. In a town whose every corner sports a coffee bar, Sinclair's stands out as a breakfast paradise with 28 different kinds of tea, serve-yourself coffee, wonderful homemade pastries, and piles of daily newspapers. In fact, it's worth a trip just to sit in one of the large windows with a steaming caffe latte and watch the fog slowly float away. On weekend mornings, Sinclair's is packed, but there are also bistro tables on the sidewalk where you can sit and observe San Francisco's yuppies loading up their Land Rovers with either sailboards or snowboards. Unlike many restaurants of this style, reservations are accepted, and there is validated parking at a Polk Street lot several blocks away.

Russian Hill

Sinclair's Le Petit Cafe, 2164 Larkin Street (at Green); (415) 776-5356. Hours: Breakfast 7:30–11:30 A.M. Tuesday–Friday; Brunch 8:30 A.M.–2:30 P.M. Saturday–Sunday; Lunch 11:30 A.M.–2:30 P.M. Tuesday–Friday; Dinner 5:30 P.M.–10 P.M. Tuesday–Saturday.

28 / The Dukes of Dungeness

Swan's Oyster Depot

There are 22 stools at the counter, and a perpetual stream of customers waits outside to get in. The front wall sports a hand-scrawled menu of the day's offerings and a huge stuffed marlin. It wasn't in any guidebook (until now), and it is so small you'd never see it unless you knew in advance. But make no mistake about it—if you've come to San Francisco to eat fish, you're in the right place!

Swan's Oyster Depot offers very simple fare: six or seven fish cocktails; clams and oysters on the half shell; Dungeness crab (their most popular item); Boston clam chowder; and four or five entrées: smoked trout ($11.25), lobster cooked to order (billed as "The Maine Attraction"—$25.00 for two), and a variety of salads (shrimp: $10.95, crab: $11.95, lobster: $14.00). Beers are standard issue and so are the wines.

But as soon as you sit down, the person on either side of you will probably ask if it's your first time, and then tell you that he or she has been coming there for 16 years. Part of the credit for this loyalty goes to the owners who are great guys and funny beyond belief (some of them even speak Brooklynese, which is amazing given that they're locals). There are six of them, six Italian brothers whose ownership goes back to 1946, when their father bought the place from four Danish brothers who had owned it since 1912. The Sancimino Brothers serve 200–300 people a day and they're closed by 5:30 P.M.

A longtime customer sums up Swan's appeal: "You can get better atmosphere" (interrupted by a bellowing "get outta here" from Tony Sancimino, who is standing at the end of the counter shucking oysters), "but no place in the Bay Area offers better fish!"

Russian Hill

Swan's Oyster Depot, 1517 Polk Street near California; (415) 673-1101. Open Monday–Saturday, 8 A.M.–5:30 P.M.

29 / Behind the Scenes at Cable Car Central

The Cable Car Barn and Museum

OK, so you've ridden them. And you probably had a great time, hanging your body out over the edge of the car, especially as it whipped around the curve. But at some point, you had to have thought to yourself, "how do these things run?" For answers to that question and more, head over to the Cable Car Barn and Museum, an 1887 brick building that serves as the very heart and soul of cable car operations.

Go first to the upstairs viewing platform where you can see the giant wheels responsible for moving the cars along the street. Cable cars have no motors or power of their own; they grip the moving cables and automatically travel along with them in much the same way as people on a ski tow. When you've had enough of this view, head downstairs to the underground viewing windows where you'll see the huge revolving sheaves (wheels with grooved rims) that guide the cables in their continuous 8½-mile circuit beneath San Francisco's streets. All cable cars are powered by cables routed through these sheaves, and all lines pass within three blocks of this building.

Now that you've done the "Barn" part of this tour, spend some time with the "Museum" part. The mezzanine houses the first cable car ever built as well as a variety of past models, cable car parts, historical photos, and an exhibit on earthquakes. There are also a number of old photos showing the horse-pulled cars that preceded today's cable-powered ones. To the left of the door as you exit the museum, note the plaque dedicated to Frieda Klussman, "The Cable Car Lady." A great tour for all ages and especially right after a cable car ride—ask the conductor to drop you off. Chances are, he'll know where it is.

Russian Hill

The Cable Car Barn and Museum, 1201 Mason Street at Washington; (415) 474-1887. Open daily 10 A.M.–5 P.M. Free admission.

30 / The Crookedest Street in the World

Lombard Street

You would think there'd be other ways of dealing with a really steep slope. But in the mid-1920s, creating a narrow zig-zaggy street with eight sharp turns on a 40-degree slope seemed like a good idea. It has turned out to be a great idea, but in a very different way than those early engineers imagined. One of San Francisco's top tourist attractions, Lombard Street—alternately known as "The World's Crookedest Street"—winds and twists down the slope between Hyde and Leavenworth streets, baffling the hordes of tourists who begin the drive along its switchbacks thinking what a wonderful experience it would be only to realize at the halfway point that they aren't sure they can make it.

The best thing is to walk, not only to erase the logistical problems created by having to negotiate a hairpin curve every 50 feet, but in order to fully appreciate the beautifully landscaped gardens that line the street. There are stairways (without curves) on each side, and you may want to pause halfway down to appreciate the wonderful view of the bay.

The second best thing is to stand at the bottom looking up at the lineup of cars proceeding down the slope at a snail's pace. What drivers generally do is queue up halfway down, waiting to have a clear line of descent in case they are unable to stop. Often, you'll see friends and family members, who have chosen not to make the drive, standing at the bottom, looking up, grinning, and taking pictures. A most unusual attraction!

Russian Hill

Lombard Street is located between Hyde and Leavenworth streets.

31 / Stairways to Heaven
Russian Hill Steps

Believe it or not, there are places in this city too steep for a sidewalk. So city parents created the next best thing to an elevator—stairways. There are over 350 of them, in all shapes and sizes, and all so perfectly situated that partway up, when totally exhausted, you can stop and claim to be taking a "view" break. Three of the best stairways are in Russian Hill.

The northward-facing Larkin Steps begin their descent at the end of Larkin Street and offer a stunningly panoramic view of everything between the Bay Bridge and the Golden Gate. That, of course, means Alcatraz and Sausalito, Ghirardelli Square and its enormous clock tower, the huge sailing ships docked near Hyde Street Pier, and if you go in the early morning, one of the most magnificent sunrises you'll ever see (unless it's foggy, in which case it'll be one of the most magnificent fog banks). The steps wind their way down to Ghirardelli Square amidst a colorful profusion of nasturtiums, violets, poppies, and edible wild fennel (very tasty in early spring).

There are two sets of Greenwich Steps. One connects Hyde with Larkin, bisects a luxuriously verdant park topped by an often-overlooked tennis court, and provides spectacular views of the Presidio and the Golden Gate. The other connects Hyde and Leavenworth and looks out over North Beach to Coit Tower. When you're strolling down through the park, note the community-constructed plastic bag holders considerately placed in areas frequented by dogs and their owners.

The Vallejo Steps face east, stretch for two blocks between Jones and Mason, and guide you past an endless series of painstakingly landscaped gardens. Along the way, you can stop at a number of "lookout points" designed for viewing Telegraph Hill, North Beach, the Financial District, and the glimmering San Francisco Bay. When you get to the bottom, it's just a few more blocks to North Beach, where you can sit down at an outdoor cafe and sip a creamy caffe con cioccolata.

Russian Hill

32 / Soaring Spires

Grace Cathedral

You should arrive at Grace Cathedral at the precise moment the 44-bell English carillon rings out its greetings. The six-ton bell is the largest of its kind in the U.S. and to hear it might remind you that the angels themselves are singing. The cathedral too, will enchant you. It's the third largest of the world's 81 Episcopal cathedrals and occupies a 2.5-acre city block. It's a special place for San Franciscans to gather for moments of public rejoicing and mourning; every New Year's Eve, musician Bobby McFerrin leads a 24-hour meditation and prayer service to offer a healing for the world's suffering.

Inspired by French and Catalan Gothic cathedrals, Grace's Ghiberti doors are exact duplicates of those on Florence's baptistry. The labyrinth replicates the stone floor pattern laid in the cathedral at Chartres in 1220. Note the magnificent rose window above the rear choir loft, and the high altar made of California granite and 2,000 year-old California redwood. Note also the colorful fresco murals along both sides of the cathedral depicting historic moments in the life of the church. If you can, come for either a music concert or during services when the organ is playing. The organ consists of 123 ranks, 7,286 pipes, five keyboards, and a pedalboard. Its sound is spectacular! After visiting the cathedral, go to Huntington Park across the street for a ray of sunshine amidst Nob Hill elegance.

Nob Hill

Grace Cathedral, 1051 Taylor Street at California; (415) 749-6300 Services are held daily (call for schedule). Tours are given Monday–Friday 1 P.M.– 3 P.M., Saturday 11:30 A.M.–1:30 P.M. and Sunday 12:30 P.M.–2 P.M. For concert information, call (415) 749-6302.

33 / Gold Star Grandeur
The Fairmont Hotel

Both San Francisco and the Fairmont trace their roots back to the 1849 California Gold Rush. The land on which the Fairmont sits was bought by "Bonanza Jim" Fair after he struck it rich and set out to claim respectability by moving into the city's most elite neighborhood. But instead of a residence, he built a European-style palace that would play host to international dignitaries, celebrities, and the crème of high society.

On the eve of the Fairmont's official debut, the 1906 earthquake rocked San Francisco, but while buildings throughout the city crumbled, the hotel's Corinthian marble columns braced against collapse. The hotel served as a command post for the mayor and city officials who sat on crated furniture in the lobby and plotted strategy to halt the inferno engulfing the city.

Today, the Fairmont is one of the city's most elegant landmarks as well as a very classy and historically significant hotel. With 600 rooms and 62 suites, including the extravagant Penthouse Suite, located in a tower overlooking the original building, the hotel is known for its emphasis on providing the comforts of home (there's even complimentary homemade chicken soup for guests who are under the weather). Its range of services include an executive business center, a fitness center, and four restaurants (including the Tonga Restaurant and Hurricane Bar with Pacific Rim cuisine, exotic drinks, nightly dancing, and dramatic thunder and rainstorm effects). The penthouse Crown Room offers 360-degree city views and a jazz club, the New Orleans Room, that features a Cajun-style appetizer menu and international cabaret superstars.

The Fairmont Hotel sits on the summit of Nob Hill, at the crossroads of the Powell, Hyde, and California cable car lines.
Nob Hill

The Fairmont Hotel, 950 Mason Street at California; (415) 772-5000 or (800) 527-4727. Rooms from $229 to $550.

34 / A Break in the Middle of the Day

Noontime Concerts in Old St. Mary's Cathedral

When they started in 1989, nobody thought they'd turn into one of the city's most cherished cultural traditions. But they soon became a noontime ritual for everyone from stockbrokers escaping the frenzy of the nearby Financial District to shoppers prowling the elegant Nob Hill boutiques. Based on models in London, Paris, Boston, and New York, the noontime concerts feature Bay Area and other touring musicians playing classical chamber music in Old St. Mary's Cathedral every Tuesday from 12:30 P.M. to 1 P.M. (why "noontime concerts" don't start at noon is anybody's guess). Contrary to what most people think, the concerts are presented by a nonprofit group of musicians funded through private donations (including the suggested $3 minimum collected at the door), not by the cathedral which simply—and graciously—provides the space.

Old St. Mary's is a quiet, unassuming sanctuary whose history dates back to 1854. Located on the southern end of Chinatown, it's called *Dai Choong Low* by the Chinese—"Tower of the Big Bell"—and forms an agreeable architectural contrast to the pagoda roofs, dragon's glow street lamps, and the cable cars that rumble by just outside its door. The church is well worth a visit, especially on Tuesdays when its vaulted interior resonates with the lyrical melodies of Chopin, Beethoven, Bach, or whatever else talented musicians have cooked up.

Nob Hill

Noontime Concerts, in Old St. Mary's Cathedral, California and Grant, are held every Tuesday at 12:30 P.M. For concert information, call (415) 288-3840.

35 / Some Enchanted Evening
Cabaret

Like other cosmopolitan cities, San Francisco contains a wealth of possibilities for those who like their music quiet, personal, and in intimate settings. Here are three of the best of the city's cabarets:

The **Plush Room**, located in the York Hotel, 940 Sutter Street, near Leavenworth, features national and international chanteuses (sometimes you'll catch a male act, but usually velvet-voiced torch-singers) in a venue befitting its name. Cover charges hover in the $10 range, and there's a two-drink minimum. Call (415) 885-2800 for showtimes.

Finocchio's, 506 Broadway at Kearney (415) 982-9388, offers a somewhat different experience. This long-established (since 1936) San Francisco institution features female impersonators in fabulous costumes performing sock 'em dead Las Vegas-style revues. Very much a tourist place, but one that delivers every bit of what it promises. Each night brings three different 75-minute shows, and the $14.50 admission entitles you to stay for all of them if you so desire. Full bar and parking next door.

Getting back to quiet and intimate, the New Orleans Room in the Fairmont Hotel, 950 Mason Street (415) 772-5000, offers tufted leather chairs, soft lighting, a Bela Lugosi–draped backdrop, and some of the best cabaret stars around. Cover charges vary but expect to pay about $20 with a two-drink minimum. Reservations necessary on weekends.

Financial District

36 / Where the Chefs Are Graded on Their Cooking

The California Culinary Academy

It's not the same thing as getting your hair permed at a hair-cutting school, believe me. Your chances of getting anything other than superb food here are virtually nonexistent. In fact, you probably wouldn't even know you were dining in a culinary academy except that you're paying rock-bottom prices for four-star food. Standards are consistently and uncompromisingly high.

The students work under the direction of master chef-instructors and although the menu changes according to what's being studied that week, the focus is on classic European cooking.

The academy is housed in historic California Hall, where diners have a choice of three restaurants. The first and most formal is the Careme Room, which has great big expanses of glass through which you can watch the students in the kitchen creating their soufflés. Here, you can get a prix fixe three-course lunch and dinner on most weekdays (the academy is closed on weekends) and a classic European buffet dinner on Friday. The Brasserie offers international lunches, and the Academy Grill—a comfortable basement bar—serves light lunches and evening appetizers.

Civic Center

The California Culinary Academy, 625 Polk Street at Turk; (415) 771-3500. The Careme Room is open for lunch sittings at noon and 12:30 P.M. and dinner sittings at 6 P.M., 6:45 P.M., and 7:30 P.M. Reservations are essential. The Brasserie is open for lunch from 11:45 A.M. to 1:15 P.M. The Academy Grill offers lunch from 11:30 A.M. to 2 P.M. and appetizers from 3 P.M. to 9 P.M. Reservations at the Brasserie or the Academy Grill are recommended. Prices are moderate and there is a full bar. Closed on weekends.

37 / Dining in a Tuscan Villa

Vivande Ristorante

The name stems from the Latin word *viva* or "life." But it also means "things to live by," which is why chef-owner Carlo Middione chose it for this very personal statement of a restaurant, which opened its doors in April 1995. First the decor: it is stunning—elegant and inviting with the warmth and graciousness of a Tuscan villa. An enormous stone statue of an open mouth serves as the entranceway and is inspired by the *Bocca della Veritá*—"Mouth of Truth"—found on a building at the top of Rome's Spanish Steps. Tradition has it that the mouth will close on the hand of anyone who, placing it there, swears a false oath. According to Middione, no limbs have yet been lost.

The food is at least equal to the decor if not better (an almost impossible achievement). Middione's creations evoke the best of southern Italian cuisine, which is the food he grew up with. Many of the recipes, in fact, are taken from his classic book, *The Food of Southern Italy*, which won the 1987 Tastemaster Award for international cooking. House specialties include vongole della casa (fresh Manila clams baked in a wood oven with white wine, garlic, saffron, parsley, and lemon); pappardelle al ragù di coniglio (handcut, house-made pappardelle pasta served with a ragù of braised rabbit and tomatoes); and branzino al forno (Chilean seabass on a bed of braised red cabbage Agrigento-style with capers, red-wine vinegar, and roasted potatoes). Get the picture? Appetizers range from $7 to $11; entrées, from $17 to $22.

Any other concerns about this 150-seat restaurant can be laid to rest by chef Carlo's own words: "I want Vivande to be a first-class restaurant that preserves a down-home approach, has good food and value, and a redefinition of four-star service. We are warmly welcoming, with zero attitude and no bad tables." Amen.
Civic Center

Vivande Ristorante, 670 Golden Gate, off Franklin and to the left of the Opera Plaza Movie Theater; (415) 673-9245, fax (415) 673-2160. Open daily, 11:30 A.M.–12 midnight. Reservations necessary on weekends.

38 / The Hallelujah Corner
Glide Memorial Church

There's only one Cecil Williams, Minister of Liberation at Glide Memorial Church, and you can catch him on Sunday mornings "talking the talk" and "walking the walk." That's how he describes the brand of liberation theology that spills from his soul and fuses effortlessly with the spontaneous testimonies, slide shows, and jazz and rock music that make up a typical Sunday service at this unique United Methodist church.

The music (provided by the Glide Choral Ensemble and accompanied by a live band) has received international acclaim and if you go, you're bound to see a combination of people from every segment of society—all races, classes, ages, sexual orientations, nationalities, and religious backgrounds—up on their feet clapping and singing. At some point during the service, you probably will join them, and you'll leave Glide Memorial feeling one with everything and everybody and ready to tackle whatever falls in your path.

On your way out, you'll be greeted by Reverend Williams and invited to a postservice breakfast held downstairs in the community cafeteria. It too is a great experience, but you also might decide that nothing can top what you've already experienced.

"Sunday" clothes are required—no shorts or sweatshirts—and a donation is appreciated.

Civic Center

Glide Memorial Church, 330 Ellis Street near Mason; (415) 771-4014. Sunday services are at 9 A.M. and 11 A.M.

39 / Placido, Luciano, and Mikhail Have All Slept Here, Too

The Inn at the Opera

Forget the fact that the guest list has included everyone from Midori to Claudia Schiffer, and that the principal dancers of the Joffrey and the American Ballet Theater stay here when they're performing nearby. Managing Director Thomas Noonan and his cast of service professionals will treat you with every bit as much deference. By way of illustrating his attention to detail, Noonan orders a block of impossible-to-get symphony, ballet, and opera tickets for guests of the hotel and—amazingly—offers them with no additional markup. ("Other hotels' concierges call us," he says.)

A small and elegant hotel, The Inn at the Opera has just 30 rooms and 18 suites. Each is decorated in pastel colors and features a queen-sized bed with canopy, oversized throw pillows, an antique armoire, a microwave oven, and a well-stocked minibar. Upon arriving, you're also treated to classical music flowing from the clock radio, a vase of fresh flowers, and a basket of red apples. (If you're in a suite, you'll also find truffles and thick floor-length bathrobes.)

And as if it weren't enough to have quiet elegant rooms and perfect service, the inn also encompasses one of the city's finest restaurants, Act IV, whose plush, clublike environment and excellent food make it the chosen eatery of opera and symphony stars performing down the street. It's also open later than most of the city's restaurants, again, in deference to the large number of performing artists and their fans who stay here.

Civic Center

The Inn at the Opera, 333 Fulton Street near the Opera House; (415) 863-8400, fax (415) 861-0821. Rooms range from $125 to $265 for a suite. Act IV is open for breakfast daily 7 A.M. to 10 A.M., for lunch Monday–Saturday 12 noon–2 P.M. and for dinner nightly 5:30 P.M.–10:30 P.M. Sunday brunch is served 11:30 A.M.–2:30 P.M. The Lounge is open 11 A.M.–1 A.M. and serves a cafe menu at the bar all day and evening.

40 / A Place Where Everybody Sings

Max's Opera Cafe

You walk into this cavernous place and think, "how nice" when you hear the piano player's ivory tinkling. But seconds after you settle down to peruse the equally cavernous menu, you'll hear someone start to belt it out à la Broadway, and when you look up, you'll find that it's the very same waiter or waitress who just handed you the menu. Welcome to Max's Opera Cafe where part of the job interview requires you to sing. Everybody who works here sings here, and the selections range from Mimi's last aria in *La Boheme* to a bluesy torched rendition of "Cry Me a River."

OK, the singing is great. But what about the food? It's good—in fact, some things are very good. But the most notable feature of this cross between New York and California deli cuisine is its abundance. From the huge burgers, enormous plates of pasta, the oversize bowl of chicken soup, or the too-much-already slice of chocolate cake, you will never leave Max's Opera Cafe hungry. You'll never leave disappointed either. And with a menu approaching the size of a small novella, it's the perfect place to go when everybody in your party wants to eat something different. A popular pre- and post-performance haunt for those attending events at the nearby Performing Arts Center, Max's crowd is a pleasant mix of jeans and evening gowns. Prices are moderate (entrées in the $13 range) and includes a full bar.

Civic Center

Max's Opera Cafe, 601 Van Ness Avenue at Golden Gate; (415) 771-7300. Open Sunday through Thursday 11:30 A.M.–midnight and Friday and Saturday from 11:30 A.M.–1:30 A.M.

41 / From Grain to Glass

San Francisco Brewing Company

The area once served as a playground for San Francisco's rough-and-tumble, gold-fevered 49ers. Dubbed the Barbary Coast, it sported dozens of rowdy saloons, where angling executives, sharp-talking politicians, and homesick sailors all rubbed elbows. Only one is still standing, the 1907 Andromeda, where boxing champion Jack Dempsey perfected his right hook while working as a bouncer in 1913.

Today it is run by Alan Paul, a former home-brewer who bought it in 1985 and renamed it the San Francisco Brewing Company, thus giving birth to the first brewpub in San Francisco and the fourth in the U.S. The saloon's most famous characteristic, aside from its beer, is the bar, which features flame mahogany columns, a beveled-glass backdrop, and an enormous overhead contraption made in 1916 of brass and palm fronds. It's called a Pukka Walla fan and it runs the entire length of the bar, powered by a tiny motor via leather belts.

The San Francisco Brewing Company produces approximately 200 mouth-watering gallons of beer per batch, or six barrels of brew at a time. Paul's knowledge and love of Barbary Coast history finds vent in the beers' colorful names: Albatross Lager, Gripman's Porter, Pony Express Ale, Andromeda Wheat Beer, Alcatraz Stout, and Emperor Norton Lager. This last is named after a wealthy businessman who went mad after losing everything in a Gold Rush deal, proclaiming himself Emperor of the U.S. and Protector of Mexico.

The brewery also serves food—hearty international fare—and a varied menu of live music. Tours of the brewing rooms are given by the staff upon request. *North Beach*

San Francisco Brewing Company, 155 Columbus Avenue at Pacific; (415) 434-3344. Open daily. Sunday, noon–11:30 P.M. (kitchen, 1 P.M.–7 P.M.); Monday–Thursday, 11:30 A.M.–12:30 A.M. (kitchen, 11:30 A.M.–3 P.M. and 5 P.M.–9 P.M.); Friday, 11:30 A.M.–1:30 A.M. (kitchen, 11:30 A.M.–10 P.M.); and Saturday, noon–1:30 A.M. (kitchen, noon–10 P.M.).

42 / Is That a Fire Nozzle on the Hill?

Coit Tower

The simple and elegant Coit Tower exists because an eccentric woman named Lillie Hitchcock-Coit left money "for the purpose of adding beauty to the city I have always loved." And so she built what has become a cherished, albeit equally eccentric, monument. Born in the early 1800s, Hitchcock-Coit smoked cigars, drank bourbon, and loved dressing up as a man to gamble in North Beach saloons. But she is best remembered for her life-long devotion to firefighting; after becoming a mascot to the Knickerbocker Hose Company 5 in 1863, she rarely missed a blaze. And so she left $125,000 to honor her beloved local fire department—a donation that ultimately found its form in the 180-foot concrete column that commands attention from its perch on grassy Telegraph Hill. But contrary to popular belief, the tower was not purposely built to look like a fire nozzle.

Coit Tower dominates San Francisco's skyline; it can be seen from almost everywhere in the city. Its ground floor also contains an astounding group of murals that were painted in 1933 by some 30 local artists, each piece depicting a different aspect of the Great Depression. But the main attraction here is the view, and it is one of the best in town. On clear days you can see Mount Diablo to the east, the Claremont Resort in the Oakland Hills, Alcatraz, Sausalito, the Golden Gate Bridge, the Presidio, and Fisherman's Wharf. The best thing to do is to park the car at the foot of the incline and walk up Telegraph Hill. The parking lot at the top is small and traffic is usually congested. But there's an elevator to the top of the tower, so don't despair.

Telegraph Hill

Coit Tower is open daily 10 A.M.–5:30 P.M. Admission is $3.

43 / Calling Fred and Ginger

Where to Have a Swingin' Time

There's something here called California Swing Dancing, and it's gotten so popular that it can be seen anywhere there's a wooden floor and an upbeat tempo. Following are four of the best places for trying out your spins and twirls.

The **Hi-Ball Lounge**, 473 Broadway, (415) 39-SWING, is done up in fire-engine red, with brick along one wall and tiger-skin print on the other. The dance floor is in front of the band-stand and it is the place to be if you want to swing. Dancing starts at 9:30 P.M. Friday and Saturday. Get there early; legal capacity is 49 and it fills quickly. On Sunday and Tuesday, Johnny "Swing" Boulland gives free swing lessons one hour before dancing begins.

The back room of the **Cafe du Nord** cellar, 2170 Market Street, (415) 979-6545, looks like a ballroom from the Texas Panhandle with two tacky chandeliers and a spotlighted curtain. But it has one of the few 12-piece big bands around playing everything from Benny Goodman to the Duke.

And on Sundays, the Fabulous Juan offers free dance lessons at 8 P.M., while men in narrow sideburns and greasy ducktails strut the floor in short sleeve shirts unbuttoned over white singlets.

The **Coconut Grove**, 1415 Van Ness, (415) 776-1616, offers the Swing Kings or the Rhythm Sheiks on Saturday, and Sina-tra knock-offs playing the standards on Monday. A glitzy old-time club with fake palm trees and plenty of dance space.

The **DNA Lounge**, 375 11th Street, (415) 626-1409, features rock-and-roll-rooted swing dancing with male dancers dressed in bowling shirts and sporting sideburns and silver wallet chains and females in flying circle skirts. Lots of tossing, shoulder and arm flips. Live music.

44 / Bohemian Charm in North Beach

Hotel Boheme

If you missed North Beach during the Beat generation, the Hotel Boheme is for you. Described by *Condé Nast Traveler* as "a high style '90s homage to the On the Road generation," this bay-windowed Victorian is a colorful reincarnation of a North Beach that in the '50s and '60s played host to alternative poets, drop-out writers, and black turtlenecked denizens of smoky cafes. You enter through black-and-gold portieres and make your way down hallways lined with a permanent gallery of black-and-white photographs evoking the Beat era—past doorways painted sage green, cantaloupe, and sweet lavender with black trim. The rooms' light fixtures are handmade from glazed collages of '50s jazz sheet music, Ginsberg poetry, old menus, and newspaper headlines.

Each of the 15 rooms has a private bath, a queen-sized iron bed, European armoire, bistro table with wicker chairs, Matisse and Picasso prints, and pillows covered with opium-poppy fabric. A clearly starstruck desk clerk reveals that when Allen Ginsberg stays here, he requests one of the rooms facing his old haunts on Columbus Avenue. Located in the heart of North Beach, the Hotel Boheme is close to everything including City Lights Bookstore, which continues to be one of the last active bastions of Beat.

North Beach

Hotel Boheme, 444 Columbus Avenue; (415) 433-9111. Doubles from $105 to 115.

45 / We're Not in Kansas, Toto

Beach Blanket Babylon

Anyone who doubts San Francisco's lock on the title of wacki-est city in the U.S. need only look to its 22-year embrace of Beach Blanket Babylon, a show that features singing poodles, dancing Christmas trees, outrageously huge hats, and an enor-mous Mr. Peanuts. There is no question of the city's love of this cabaret-style pop culture spoof that is now the longest running, biggest hit musical revue in theater history. It surpassed the "Ziegfield Follies" in 1984 and gave its 7,547th performance December 31, 1995. Beach Blanket Babylon continually evolves in its hilarious parodies of popular icons (like having Anita Hill sing "Respect" to Clarence Thomas with a Supreme Court cho-rus), updating its targets and adding new characters, songs, and send-ups every year. Previous hit incarnations have included: the 1983 "Beach Blanket Babylon Goes to London" (Maggie Thatcher got to wear a huge pineapple hat), the 1984 "Beach Blanket Babylon Goes to the Prom," and the 1985 "Beach Blan-ket Babylon's Makin' Whoopee." In the current version, Snow White looks for love in all the wrong places and is comforted in her "recovery" by a cast of therapeutically New Age dwarfs.

This intrepid revue takes place in North Beach's Club Fugazi and is characterized by a frenzied pace, a raucous sound level, and a persistent gag-a-second style. It doesn't get any crazier than this!

North Beach

Beach Blanket Babylon, at Club Fugazi, 678 Green Street; (415) 421-4222. Wednesday–Thursday, 8 P.M. $23–40; Friday–Saturday, 7 P.M. and 10 P.M. $26–45; and Sunday 3 P.M. and 7 P.M. $18–37. Advance reser-vations necessary.

46 / Great Cheap Food in North Beach

Pasta Pomodoro

Forget any prejudices you may have about cheap pasta places. This place is very, very good. All the pasta is freshly made on the premises. If you get a table at the back, near the work station, you'll see the cooks reaching into any of 20-or-so drawers depending on which order they're working on. Amazingly, each order is prepared individually.

Let's say you select penne puttanesca, which is penne made with black olives, capers, anchovies, garlic, spicy tomatoes, and parmesan cheese. The cook will reach into the penne drawer, pull out a portion, and place it in boiling water. Then he'll take a handful of each of the other ingredients, throw them in a skillet, and cook the sauce in a flamboyant style that involves flipping the ingredients into the air a few times. Four minutes later, when the penne are done, he'll drain and add them to the skillet, and then, presto, onto a dish and to your table. Each skillet cooks one dish; when the cook is done with yours, he sends the skillet to the dishwasher and takes a clean one.

With such individual attention, you might thing this place holds maybe 10 or 12 people. Wrong. There's room for about 80, with approximately 30 of the seats placed around a horseshoe-shaped bar used mainly by local singles. The decor echoes an Italian theme: red-, green-, and white-tiled floor; cans of tomatoes and olive oil displayed on counters; and large mirrors painted with tomatoes, peppers, and scenes from Italy.

The prices: cheap. Top pasta price is $6.50—for fish linguine with bay scallops, lemon, tomato, basil, and spices. The bulk of the pastas are around $5. There's even a polenta with fontina cheese and tomatoes that's $3.75. The menu also features salads, sandwiches, desserts, wines, and beers. Amazing!

North Beach

Pasta Pomodoro, 655 Union at Columbus; (415) 399-0300. Open daily 11 A.M.–11 P.M. Cash only.

47 / "A Fascinating Experience Is in Your Future"

The Golden Gate Fortune Cookie Factory

The first thing you see when you walk into this odd little place is the pileup of clear plastic bags filled with crisp golden fortune cookies. There must be hundreds of bags, each filled with hundreds of cookies. Then you notice the four women, each sitting in front of what look like miniature pancake griddles moving in front of them with assembly-line speed. A mechanical siphon pours cookie batter onto each tiny griddle at the beginning of the line, and then the griddles move on a rotating belt, through an oven, until finally reaching the women, who remove the cooked pancakes, stuff them with fortunes, fold them in half, and then curl them into the familiar fortune-cookie shape. Among the four of them, the women produce 25,000 cookies a day. Half are stuffed with the banal fortunes you get at the end of every Chinese meal. The other half—the ones printed on yellow paper—are called French Adult Fortunes and are sold to restaurants desiring a slightly spicier version of the future.

The factory belongs to Franklin Yee, who has owned it for 31 years. Visitors are welcome to watch, and you're even more welcome if you buy a tourist-sized bag of the just-baked cookies ($4 for either the regular or the French Adult version). After you're done here, you might consider getting a haircut next door in the one-seat Chinese barbershop whose front window is covered with photos of Hollywood stars. There's Michael Douglas, Clint Eastwood, Robert Conrad, and a host of others who presumably had their locks pruned here.

Chinatown

The Golden Gate Fortune Cookie Factory, 56 Ross Alley (between Grant and Stockton). Open daily 10 A.M.–7 P.M.

48 / Old-World Charmer

Hotel San Remo

There are bigger, more luxurious, more centrally located, and more high-profile hotels. But it's hard to find one more endearing than this delightful little three-story Italianate Victorian hidden away between bustling Washington Square and Fisherman's Wharf. What's more, you won't believe the price—$45 for a single and $85 for the penthouse suite. If you're already thinking, sure, but what do I have to compromise, think again. The small, tidy rooms are reminiscent of those in English bed and breakfasts with iron beds, feathery comforters, mounds of fluffy pillows, pedestal sinks, wicker furniture, rag rugs, and maple dressers. Most also have ceiling fans. There are 62 of them, laid out along long winding corridors awash with antiques, leaded glass windows, stained glass skylights, and endless pots of robust philodendrons. All rooms share the spotless bath facilities that include Victorian tile floors, brass pull-chain toilets, oak tanks, and clawfoot tubs, as well as showers. The penthouse suite, however, has a private bath as well as a small deck and a 360-degree view of the city.

The owner, Tom Field, and his excellent city-savvy staff are always ready with suggestions when asked, for instance, for a funky little coffee shop within a two-block radius, or an elegant Italian restaurant that serves vegetarian fare. Let's face it, you could spend a lot more. Or you could park your bags at the Hotel San Remo and pat yourself on the back for having snagged a great find.

North Beach

Hotel San Remo, 2337 Mason Street (at Chestnut); (415) 776-8688. $45–65 single; $55–75 double; $85 for the penthouse.

49 / An Istrian Restaurant in North Beach

Albona

Food buffs in constant quest of new and different cuisines will love Albona, where Bruno Viscovi and his wife, Rae, have lovingly recreated the food of his native Istria. The Istrian Peninsula juts into the northern end of the Adriatic Sea. For nearly 2,000 years, it was part of Italy, and its history is closely aligned with the rise of the Venetian Empire. Later, it became a way-station for traders returning from Constantinople, and its northern Italian cuisine expanded to include ingredients from the East—almonds, raisins, cinnamon, saffron, and nutmeg. By the fourteenth century, Austria-Hungary had become the dominant power in this region, and the food expanded again to include central European influences, such as pork dishes, goulash, sauerkraut, and strudel. At the end of World War II, Istria was ceded to Yugoslavia and today forms part of Croatia. Its food reflects its past, with a combination of influences that include Italian, Greek, Turkish, Jewish, French, Austrian, Hungarian, and Slav.

Albona is named after the hillside town where Bruno lived until 1951, when he immigrated to San Francisco. Its distinctive menu features the foods of his youth and includes such marvels as Crafi Albonese, crescent-shaped pasta puffs filled with three cheeses, pine nuts, and raisins, and served with a pungent sirloin meat sauce laced with cumin. All the desserts, from apple strudel to chocolate ricotta torte, are made in-house; the wine list features vintages from the Friuli region of northern Italy.

Albona's interior is as satisfying as its menu—a small cozy dining room with mahogany wainscoting and long beveled mirrors hung alongside photos of Albona and maps of the Istrian peninsula. Entrées are in the $15 range.

North Beach

Albona, 545 Francisco Street between Taylor and Mason; (415) 441-1040. Dinner Tuesday through Saturday, 5 P.M.–10 P.M. Major credit cards accepted; complimentary valet parking.

50 / Spend Some Time in North Beach's Living Room

Washington Square

Madrid has its Plaza Mayor, Moscow has Red Square, and Boston has the Commons. Each is a good place to go to get the feel of that particular city; to see the people and the buildings and the relationships that define what life is really like there. Although San Francisco is too diverse to have just one such gathering place, Washington Square is a good place to go if you want to understand North Beach. For starters, it's right in the center of that entertaining neighborhood—a wide open green space used by the community as a kind of outdoor living room. Neighborhood residents come to the park to sunbathe, read their papers, play Frisbee, picnic with their families, or practice tai chi. On Sundays, there's the extra-added attraction of artists selling their work on the park's perimeter.

Like any other important piazza, Washington Square is bordered by many of the absolute requisites. There's a post office, a library, a bakery that sells different kinds of focaccia, Malvina's Cafe, a longtime writer's hangout called the Washington Square Bar and Grill, and even one of San Francisco's new bathroom kiosks (they're self-cleaning and look like European metro entrances). If you're lucky, you'll even catch a wedding entourage crowding the steps of Saints Peter and Paul, the beautiful dual-spired, snowy white church that towers over the square.

Go when it's sunny. Pick up an ice cream cone from the nearby Ben & Jerry's (just up the block on Columbus), and lie back on the lush green grass as North Beach swirls around you in all its kaleidoscopic finery.

North Beach

Washington Square is bordered by Union, Columbus, Filbert, and Stockton streets.

51 / A Three-Star Hole in the Wall

House of Nanking

Whoever came up with the term *dive* must have had this place in mind. It's a long, narrow room with tables crowded so close that it's impossible not to hear even the most intimate of sweet nothings and that the windows are spattered with cooking grease. But the food is out of this world, and the restaurant is consistently rated with three stars. In fact, if you look around at the walls, you'll see dozens of citations testifying to the fact that this is one of the finest Chinese restaurants in the region.

The best place to sit is at the counter, where you can watch the chef do his thing. Moving a mile a minute, he flips fresh prawns in a sesame-coated wok with one hand while battering succulent chicken nuggets with the other. Each dish is prepared on the spot, individually, with its own set of ingredients (bright purple eggplant, fat green beans, long slender asparagus).

The restaurant is the brainchild of owner Peter Fang, who gave up a medical practice in Shanghai to pursue his lifelong dream of becoming a chef. Years ago, he did all the cooking himself, but now he has three trained disciples who carry on the tradition. The food is amazingly fresh—Peter and his wife shop for the ingredients every morning at 6 A.M.—and the day's menu depends on what they find.

After years of long lines out the door, Nanking recently expanded into the space next door, and Peter now moonlights as a maitre d' and client adviser—if you want to really eat well, just ask him to bring whatever good dishes they're making that day. Cheap, cheap, cheap.

North Beach

House of Nanking, 919 Kearny Street between Jackson and Columbus; (415) 421-1429. Open Monday–Saturday 12 noon–10 P.M.; 4 P.M.–10 P.M. on Sunday.

52 / On a Clear Day, You Can See Forever

Three Great Viewing Points

If gorgeous views are what you're looking for, you've come to the right city. Here are three great places, each with a different perspective.

It might seem a little unorthodox but if you want an unparalleled 360-degree view of the cityscape—Coit Tower, Russian Hill, Nob Hill, and the Financial District (including the Transamerica Pyramid)—head for the rooftop of the **Vallejo Street Garage**, 766 Vallejo, between Stockton and Powell. This wonderful municipal parking garage is located right in the center of North Beach and, by the way, offers the lowest parking rates around. Take the stairway up to the roof and prepare to be overwhelmed.

Alamo Square, in the Hayes Valley, between Fulton and Hayes, Steiner and Scott, is an historic district and wonderful park bordered by exquisitely maintained Victorian homes. The 700 block of Steiner Street contains a group of particularly gorgeous Victorians known as Postcard Row because it's one of the most photographed stretches of houses in the city. From the park's summit, you get a 360-degree view of San Francisco's urban neighborhoods with the Financial District and the bay backing the eastern vista.

The top of **Fillmore and Broadway**, at the summit of Pacific Heights, offers possibly the best view of the bay available. On clear days, you can see Angel Island, Sausalito, the Golden Gate Bridge, and Alcatraz. On foggy days, you may not see as much, but you won't mind a bit because the view of the fog shrouding the bridge will thoroughly enchant you.

North Beach

53 / Dine with a Cable Car View

Zax

Zax is one of those neighborhood restaurants that you wish were in your neighborhood. It's mom-and-pop gourmet food served in a small (49 seats including two cozy window tables), serene gray-and-apricot room on the Powell-Mason cable car line. The menu emphasizes simple California-Mediterranean preparations and seasonal food that you know is fresh because the chef-owners— husband and wife team Mark Drazek and Barbara Mulas—do all the produce shopping themselves at Berkeley's wonderful Monterey Market.

Recent sample menus have included grilled New York steak with anchovy olive butter and roast rabbit with a ragout of artichokes, new potatoes, chanterelles, braised garlic, and prosciutto. Their most famous appetizer is probably the twice-baked goat cheese soufflé with apple, celery, fennel salad, and cider vinaigrette. Desserts are wonderful, and the small wine list shows knowledge and creativity. Prices range from $5 to $7 for appetizers; from $13 to $16 for entrées.

Mark and Barbara met after each decided they wanted to cook more than anything else and enrolled at the California Culinary Academy. It was love at first sight. Says Barbara, "We started keeping a list of what we wanted out of life almost as soon as we became a couple. One item that always appeared was our desire to open a small, intimate restaurant where we could keep a constant check on the level of excellence."

One visit to Zax will show you they succeeded.

North Beach

Zax, 2330 Taylor Street at Columbus, 3 blocks from Fisherman's Wharf and on the Mason-Powell cable car Line; (415) 563-6266. Open for dinner Tuesday through Saturday 5:30 P.M.–10 P.M. Reservations necessary on weekends.

54 / The Quintessential North Beach Coffeehouse

Caffe Trieste

If you've got a thing for the Beats, hurry over to this North Beach mainstay, where the chairs were once warmed by the likes of Ginsberg, Kerouac, and Ferlinghetti. Their spirit is still here, preserved by the Giotta family, who try their best to keep the place the "way it was," which, of course, means they're not keen on tourists (don't be deterred, just don't walk in waving a travel guide).

The walls are cluttered with scenes of old North Beach interspersed with glossies of opera stars, film personalities, and Trieste regulars, past and present. The coffee's good, but it's probably better in lots of other places; the pastries and the pizza look and taste like old cardboard. You're here solely for the ambience, don't forget that. To really blend in, wear something interestingly low-key (the Trieste look is an eclectic mix of rumpled clothing and little gold-rimmed glasses), and sit hunched over your table reading and writing passionately. Take your cue from Francis Ford Coppola, who hid in a corner for three months working on the *Godfather III* script.

When you can do so unobtrusively, saunter over and check out the jukebox. Trieste has probably the world's quirkiest jukebox selections—definitely skewed toward ancient opera and old-time Italian torch singers. There are also occasional Saturday afternoon concerts, where the whole Giotta family sings and customers dance in the aisles. When Yolanda, Mistress of Eclairs, comes on for "O Sole Mio," the crowd goes wild.

North Beach

Caffe Trieste, 609 Vallejo Street at Grant Avenue; (415) 788-3779. Open daily 11 A.M.–midnight.

55 / Culture on the Hoof

Guided Walking Tours

There are as many ways to see San Francisco's sights as there are sights to see. One good way is to take an organized tour. The following list contains some of the more interesting.

Chinatown Adventures Chef/author Shirley Fong-Torres ("The Wok Wiz") and her team of gastronomes help you trace Chinatown's history, folklore, and, most of all, food. Unique, informative, and very funny. (415) 355-9657.

City Art Tours pairs visitors with fine art consultant Sally Cote for a behind-the-scenes tour of the city's most exciting current art exhibitions. Tour participants get to talk with gallery directors and curators. (415) 928-8864.

Cruisin' the Castro View this gay mecca from an historical perspective as divined by Trevor Hailey. Visit the Castro Theater, AIDS Memorial Quilt Museum, and Harvey Milk's camera shop. Tuesday–Saturday 10 A.M.–1:30 P.M., brunch included and reservations required. (415) 550-8110.

Aching to relive SF's 1960s hippie movement? Then join the **Flower Power Haight-Ashbury Tour** and learn about the "Summer of Love" (the summer of 1967), as well as the Haight's past as a Victorian resort destination. Two-hour tour Tuesday–Saturday, 9:30 A.M. (415) 221-8442.

Glorious Food Culinary Walktours highlight the culinary heritage of North Beach, Chinatown, the Embarcadero waterfront, and the Ferry Plaza Farmer's Market area. Led by chef Ruby Tom and lasting approximately two hours including much noshing. (415) 441-5637.

Helen's Walk Tour gives you a highly personal (and highly rated) introduction to the city's quirky charms. Two-hour or 3½-hour grand tour of select neighborhoods. Reservations crucial. (510) 524-4544.

And finally there's **Javawalk**, which offers you a little walking and a lot of coffee. Explores San Francisco's coffee roots and coffeehouse culture from an insider perspective. Tuesday–Saturday 10 A.M.–noon. (415) 673-WALK.

56 / A Shopper's Mecca

Union Square

The hub of San Francisco's upscale shopping district is a well-manicured, 2.6-acre plot planted with palms, Irish yews, boxwood, and bright flowers. Like Paris's Place Vendor, Union Square is surrounded by smart stores and fine hotels and has at its center, a towering statue-topped column. Its name derives from a series of violent pro-Union demonstrations staged here on the eve of the Civil War.

Architecturally, the square's chief attraction is the distinctive yellow brick structure housing the Circle Gallery at 140 Maiden Lane. Designed by Frank Lloyd Wright in 1949, the building with its spiral interior ramp served as a prototype for his Guggenheim Museum in New York City.

For shopping, Union Square is right up there with Fifth Avenue, Michigan Avenue, and Rodeo Drive as one of the nation's four highest-dollar shopping meccas. Its few surrounding blocks contain not only some of the most famous names in San Francisco merchandising, but outposts of stores whose home turf lie in Paris, Milan, London, Dallas, and Tokyo.

Sak's Fifth Avenue, on the corner of Powell and Post, stands as a masterpiece of design as well as a repository of high fashion. Further down Post sits Bullock and Jones, reminiscent of fine old British clothing establishments and catering to the older man or the conservative younger one. Scheuer Linens on Stockton carries luxurious imported items. On the corner of Post and Stockton, there's Alfred Dunhill Ltd., the worldwide purveyor of cigars, pipe tobacco, and leather goods. Shreve & Co. on the corner of Post and Grant, represents the West Coast equivalent of Tiffany's. Other shopping jewels in and around Union Square include the venerable Brooks Brothers, Chanel, Hermes, Gucci, Neiman-Marcus, I. Magnin, and Laura Ashley.

Union Square

Union Square is bordered by Powell, Geary, Stockton, and Post streets.

57 / First Thing in the Morning
Three Wonderful Breakfast Spots

The locals maintain that San Francisco owns breakfast. Spend a few mornings here and you'll know why. People obviously work here, but you wouldn't know it watching them while away the hours at quaint little cafe tables sipping cappuccinos and reading the local rag. In true San Francisco style, there is an amazingly wide variety of places for you to begin the day.

For example, if you're a person who just can't start the day without a paper, you'll feel right at home at **Cafe de la Presse**, 352 Grant Street, (415) 398-2680, which carries newspapers and magazines from a dozen countries. Located near the Italian Cultural Center, the World Affairs Council, and the French Consulate, the Cafe's international flavor is reflected in its offerings. It opens at 7 A.M. each day.

If you need solitude more than a flood of information, try **Pier 40 Roastery and Cafe** where you can get a good cup of coffee; a great pastry, such as pain au chocolat; and a calm, quiet view of the bay lapping against the shore and the Embarcadero's swaying palm trees. Heartier dishes include thick slices of hazelnut French toast and a variety of omelets including one with Jack cheese and chipotle peppers. The cafe opens at 7 A.M. daily and is located south of Market at the foot of Towsend Street; (415) 495-3815.

But if you opened your eyes craving elegance, then get thee to the **Clift Hotel's French Room**. Grand vases gushing with flowers, diamond-sparkling chandeliers, fine linen tablecloths, and Louis-something chairs. You get the picture. The food is just as classy. Oven-baked crepes served with puffs of maple ricotta and a jewel-like crown of fresh berries. Buttermilk waffles with figs and apricots. Yum. There's also a Japanese breakfast, with bowls of soup, rice, crisp-crusted salmon, and marinated vegetables.

Union Square

58 / Music, Music, Music

The Virgin Records Megastore

Picture 53,000 square feet packed with over 125,000 CDs, row after row of music videos and laser discs, a multimedia area with all kinds of computers to play with, a book department, and a great cafe. Too much to visualize? Then head over to the world's largest music emporium and prepare to spend more than just an hour or two. This place is so large and so all-encompassing that they really should have thought of having motorized carts to ferry you around: "Rhythm and Blues Section, bus now boarding." Listening stations are everywhere, and you can spend hours just moving from one to the other, clamping on the headphones and floating to nirvana. Many of the music genres are even in their own enclosed space so that you can browse through jazz while listening to the likes of Bird, Miles, or Monk. Truly a feast for every palate, this place is the epitome of what PR people had in mind when they coined the phrase "Seeing Is Believing."

Union Square

The Virgin Records Megastore, Stockton Street at Market (2 blocks from Union Square); (415) 397-4525. Open Monday–Thursday 8 A.M.–11 P.M., Friday and Saturday til midnight, and Sunday 9 A.M.–11 P.M.

59 / Riding a National Landmark

San Francisco's Beloved Cable Cars

It seems incredible that San Francisco ever imagined life without them. After all, the Smithsonian-style cable cars had been named a national historic landmark in 1964. And yet, in 1982, when engineering studies showed that after 109 years of service, the cable cars had deteriorated beyond repair, and that rebuilding would cost over $60 million, the city's governing elders decided to put them in mothballs. But wisdom prevailed in the person of Frieda Klussman, "The Cable Car Lady," who forced a public vote on the issue. The results said it all: the public voted 10 to 1 to do whatever it took to save the cable cars.

The rehabilitation, which took two years, ended in mid-1984 and on the appointed day, crowds lined the tracks to witness the jaunty centenarians parading into another century of service.

Today there are 39 cable cars: 28 of the "single-enders," which ply the two Powell Street routes, and 11 of the "double-enders" which serve California Street. The former have one set of grips and are reversed on turntables; the latter have grips front and back, permitting them to move in either direction. The fleet carries 9.6 million passengers a year, and each car can carry 60–70 passengers—that's before you add in tourists hanging off the sides.

There is no better way of sampling San Francisco's sweeping vistas than by cable car. The Powell-Mason line originates at the corner of Powell and Market streets and proceeds up over Nob Hill and then down again to Fisherman's Wharf. The Powell-Hyde line—which offers the most spectacular views—runs from the same downtown intersection up over Nob and Russian hills to its turntable in Victorian Park on the northern waterfront. The California line starts at Market and California and goes over Nob Hill, crossing over the other two lines, and terminating at Van Ness. Cable cars are part of the Municipal Railway's 1,066-mile public-transport system and can be boarded at existing bus stops as well as at terminus points. Fare is $2 one way.

Union Square

60 / Doorman, Get Me a Cable Car

Villa Florence

It's not a queen or even a princess; a duchess will do to describe this gracious, well-situated hotel that offers just the right combination of price and location. The lobby is elegant, with wood-burning fireplaces, murals of Florentine scenes, and vases of fresh flowers everywhere. The 180 bedrooms are spacious, with high ceilings and country-home chic. Amenities include coffee-makers, hair dryers, and refrigerators in each room.

But the main reason for staying here is Villa Florence's proximity to many of the city's tourist attractions, including fashionable Union Square, which is just around the corner. The Powell Street cable car stops right in front of the door, and, if you've been there, done that, in 10 minutes you can walk to the Moscone Center, the Center for the Arts, Chinatown, the Embarcadero, and numerous other locations.

Another plus is Kuleto's Restaurant, located within the hotel itself. Beautifully decorated by San Francisco's most famous restaurant designer, Pat Kuleto, this upscale eatery serves northern Italian food with a new twist—wonderful original pasta, spit-roasted meats, pizzas cooked in a wood-burning stove, and an ever-changing menu of fresh fish.

Union Square

Villa Florence, 225 Powell Street just off Union Square; (415) 397-7700, fax (415) 397-1006. Rooms range from $155–$175, suites from $185–$285.

61 / Giorgio Armani and Sautéed Duck Breast

Campton Place Hotel Fashion Luncheons

Imagine yourself sitting in an elegantly appointed, peach-hued, and sunlit dining room feasting on carpaccio of venison while a parade of beautiful models waltzes continuously by your table. "The blouse is silk and the jacket, brushed linen," one murmurs softly when you express interest in the perfect little ensemble adorning her skyscraper frame. "Wear it by day as is, or by night, with just a hint of additional jewelry."

Such is the agenda at Campton Place's Fashion Luncheons, held every Saturday during fashion season (fall and spring). Each Saturday is exclusively devoted to one designer—Armani, Versace, Calvin Klein, Gucci, and Chanel are seasonal participants. Models exhibit anywhere from 40 to 75 outfits during the 1½ hour repast, and if you're like me, you'll spend much of that time wondering how it is possible for them to change so quickly and so often and still always come out looking perfect.

Campton Place is a perfect venue for these luncheons, located just steps up from fashion-conscious Union Square and combining the small niceties of a European inn with the polished precision of a grand hotel. Its restaurant is frequently ranked as one of America's best, and the hotel was recently given very high marks by *Travel & Leisure*.

Luncheons consist of three excellent courses prepared by Chef Todd Humphries who *Gourmet Magazine* calls "a trailblazer." Order the caramelized red banana tart with rum and lime for dessert—you're never going to look like those models anyway.

Union Square

Campton Place Hotel Fashion Luncheons, 340 Stockton Street at Union Square; (415) 781-5555, fax (415) 955-5536. Fashion Luncheons are held on Saturdays 12:30 P.M.–2 P.M. during fashion season (spring and fall). Three-course prix fixe luncheons are $29.

62 / Old World Elegance in a Modern Setting

The Warwick Regis Hotel

Some people like clean lines, sharp corners, uncluttered space, and everything reeking of modern. Others prefer opulent surroundings, historic sensibilities, and an immutable aura of old-world elegance. If you find yourself leaning more toward the latter when looking for a place to bed down, try this stylish nineteenth-century hotel with 80 rooms and suites furnished with Louis XVI French antiques, half-canopied beds, and scalloped drapes. Some suites have fireplaces, and the bathrooms are Italian marble with brass fixtures.

The concierge, who is as old world as the hotel, has extensive knowledge of the city and a noticeable desire to help you enjoy your trip. Best of all, the hotel is right in the middle of the theater district and—when you get that uncontrollable urge to spend lots of money—within easy strolling distance of Union Square. Moreover, if you come back too tired to even think of haute cuisine, you can drag yourself into the lobby bar, located just inside the hotel, for a snack and a nightcap.

Union Square

The Warwick Regis Hotel, 490 Geary Street between Mason and Taylor; (415) 928-7900 or (800) 82 REGIS. Fax (415) 441-8788. Rooms range from $95 to $205 for the Executive Suite.

63 / Take a Walk Along the Street of Four Faces

Grant Avenue

Grant Avenue, San Francisco's oldest artery, has had three names. Nowadays it has four faces. Originally named Calle de la Fundacion (street of the founding), its name was changed in 1846 to Dupont Street to honor an American admiral. In the late 1800s it was changed again, this time to honor the 18th American president, Ulysses S. Grant.

Grant begins its 1.6-mile gambol from Market Street to Pier 39 in high fashion. The avenue's tree-shaded walkway is scented with fresh flowers from nearby stands, and shoppers stroll through some of the city's finest specialty shops. An alley with considerable charm and a bawdy past intersects Grant between Geary and Post. Before becoming a genteel restaurant and shopping mall a few decades ago, Maiden Lane was the Barbary Coast's most lurid red-light district.

At Bush Street, the avenue abruptly changes face. On the north side of the intersection, an ornamental, green-tiled gate marks the frontier of the biggest Chinese stronghold this side of Taiwan. Here begin the calligraphic street signs and dragon-entwined lamp posts that run the eight-block length of Chinatown's main stem.

Chinatown officially ends at the three-way intersection of Grant, Columbus, and Broadway (the city's irrepressible, neon-emblazoned nightlife strip). Grant resumes on the far side of Columbus Avenue as part of what has long been the local pasta-panettone belt. Once Bohemian, then Beat, the 1200–1500 blocks have also always been home to such venerable Italian mainstays as Caffe Trieste, Figoni Hardware, and R. Iacopi and Company. Italian Grant ends at Filbert. From there to the Embarcadero, where it plunges into the bay, it features block after block of traditional Telegraph Hill dwellings—stuccoed, shingled, and wood framed, with bay windows and rising rents.

Financial District

64 / Check Your Steak Knife at the Door

Aqua

For a city as tied to the water as this one, you'd think there would be great seafood restaurants everywhere. But there are not, which is why Aqua made such a big splash when it opened in 1991. The excellence of the food probably also had a tiny bit to do with it. Aqua is a four-star restaurant with a clear mission and a distinct air of seriousness. No broiled-in-butter mainstays here. Ditto for fried fish with chips. One of the youngest chefs to run a world-class restaurant, 28-year-old Michael Mina's philosophy is "keep it simple and let the fresh flavor of the fish shine through."

He changes the menu five or six times a year to reflect seasonal availability, but all dishes are a refinement of California cuisine with French overtones. Witness the saddle of monkfish served in a pool of cumin on a plate dotted with drops of pomegranate syrup. Or the ahi tuna layered with crisp potato pancakes, spinach, and foie gras placed atop a pinot noir sauce. First courses run from $10 to $20 and entrées from $23 to $32. The wine list received the 1995 Wine Spectator Award of Excellence.

The 120-seat restaurant continues the California-French theme. From the street, Aqua's presence is announced by an 11-foot-high, white maple and glass door set with a distinctive bronze fishtail door handle. Inside, there's a 32-foot-long bar with white maple seats covered in natural Belgian linen. Two museum-size dining room mirrors reflect the warm, elegant colors of the high-ceilinged room, and the aura is enhanced by the mammoth floral decorations. Dress up for this one and bring your credit card. Very expensive, but well worth it.

Financial District

Aqua, 252 California Street near Battery. Call (415) 956-9662 or fax (415) 956-5229. Open for lunch Monday–Friday 11:30 A.M.–2:30 P.M. and dinner Monday–Thursday 5:30 P.M.–10:30 P.M. and Friday and Saturday 5:30 P.M.–11:30 P.M. Closed Sunday. Smoking in bar and lounge area only.

65 / Public Spaces in Unusual Places

Three Rooftop Gardens

On warm sunny days, San Francisco's briefcase-toters often opt for lunchtime breaks in one of the downtown area's numerous public gardens. Following are a few of the best to sample when your feet simply need a rest from all that walking.

For people watching, head for the Rooftop Garden at Crocker Galleria, 1 Montgomery Street (at Market). Planted with impatiens and carefully trimmed hedges, the garden is dotted with private sitting areas and plenty of shade trees. From here, you can survey the action on Market Street from the southeast corner, near the huge explorer-era sundial compass. Take the elevator to the third level and follow the signs.

For truly lofty views, try rising to the 15th floor of the Crown Zellerbach Building, 343 Sansome Street, where you'll find the Sun Terrace, a shady quiet rooftop garden open to the public. There are 16 trees rooted in enormous planters, each encircled by white benches. The view is magnificent: slivers of the bay peak through neighboring skyscrapers to the east, and a full-length view of the Transamerica Pyramid can be seen to the west.

Yerba Buena Gardens is located between Mission and Howard, and Third and Fourth streets. The gardens are planted on top of the underground Moscone Convention Center and are divided into three equally splendiferous parks: The Esplanade with its 5½ acres of flora, including the aromatic "Butterfly Garden" in its northeast corner; The Sister Cities Garden, which is home to flowering plants from San Francisco's 13 international sister cities, as well as a 22-foot-high waterfall cascading from a 200-foot-wide reflecting pool; and The East Garden, one-half acre of lush intimate greenery with a three-tiered fountain tucked between the two buildings belonging to the Center for the Arts.

Financial District

66 / Landmark Food in a Historic Building

Boulevard Restaurant

Consistently ranked as one of San Francisco's three best restaurants, Boulevard serves as an elegant tribute to what its designer and co-owner, Pat Kuleto, calls "everything I've ever loved about French bistros rolled into one." It's Kuleto's 153rd restaurant, his ninth in San Francisco, but the first where he felt free to truly play out his fantasies. He's taken the 1889 French-style Audiffred Building, with its Eiffel-style steel girders supporting an antique brick-paved vaulted roof, and added dark wood wainscoting, large romantic windows overlooking the Bay Bridge, terra cotta colors, and his signature subdued lighting, and created a restaurant that fills you with pleasure before you've ordered your first course.

Kuleto's partner in this venture is Nancy Oakes, who was the former owner and chef of the city's widely acclaimed L'Avenue Restaurant. Her cooking style here is a combination of American and European flavors and produces big, dazzling plates filled with the freshest organic produce, the most perfect meat and fish entrées, and the lushest, most creative desserts seen this side of Paradise. Her signature entrées include maple-cured pork loin stuffed with porcini mushrooms and served with white truffle polenta, and grilled salmon served on chive mashed potatoes, black chanterelle and hedgehog mushrooms, asparagus, and mustard sauce. Boulevard is also known for its excellent and extensive wine list. Count on spending $75 per person with wine and dessert.

Financial District

Boulevard Restaurant, 1 Mission Street at Steuart; (415) 543-6084. Open for lunch Monday–Friday 11:30 A.M.–2 P.M. Bistro food is served Monday–Friday 2 P.M.–5:15 P.M. Dinner is served daily 5:30 P.M.–10:30 P.M.

67 / Swellegant Dining

Cypress Club

Its spirited and unconventional decor can be best summed up by architect Jordan Mozer: "A restaurant should have a personality, like a friend. Every time you go there, you should see something new." Six years after opening to rave reviews, the Cypress Club remains a perfect example of Mozer's philosophy. A voluptuous wonderland of brass-and-copper archways, curvy velvet chairs, and a colorful WPA-style regional mural, the restaurant is still wowing critics with style elements such as the entry door puffed up like an old airplane wing, the coat cabinet shaped like an old television set, or—most definitely—the endomorphic, cigar-shaped marble beams and six-foot-wide parachuting doughnut chandeliers.

But as wonderful as the decor may be, it is the food that keeps people coming. That and the wine list, which is one of the finest in the world (the cellar holds approximately 14,000 bottles). Chef Alan McLennan takes traditional French cuisine to new heights here by reinventing the classics using intense flavors and elegant presentations. His signature dishes include smoked duck and leek ravioli with tomato broth and potato matchsticks, tandoor roasted loin of lamb with lyonnaise potatoes and endive salad, and a tower of foie gras with arugula, sweetcorn, and twenty-five-year-old sherry vinaigrette.

The desserts are equally impressive: pumpkin tiramisú with rum Anglaise, valrhona chocolate crème brûlée, chocolate profiterole with coconut fudge ice cream—and just like the appetizers and entrées, their presentation is as perfect as their taste.

As if the decor, food, and wine were not enough to lure you, Cypress Club also charms with its service—attentive, knowledgeable, and alert. Suavely subtle jazz trios serenade the diners. Swellegant perfection. Entrées in the $20 range.

Financial District

Cypress Club, 500 Jackson Street near Columbus; call (415) 296-8555 or fax (415) 296-9250. Sunday–Thursday 5:30 P.M.–10 P.M. and Friday and Saturday 5:30 P.M.–11 P.M.

68 / A Good Place to Wear Your Black Turtleneck and Slanted Beret

Cafe Bastille

The location gets you right in the mood—a narrow little alley-way groaning with the sounds of a tormented sax. You find the address and stick your head through the two swinging saloon doors pasted with the menu of the day. The waiter beckons you to come in—his voice is breathy and his accent, very French.

You walk into the room and voilà! You're suddenly on the Rue de Bourgogne in Montmartre, in a little neighborhood bistro, about to sit down with a glass of merlot and a bowl of hearty onion soup. You'll take your time, of course, and savor each of the distinctive flavors, rolling each morsel around on your tongue, promising to remember to tell so-and-so about this fabulous new place you've discovered.

As you muse, your eyes will become riveted on the musicians playing at the other side of the long, rectangular room. It might be blues, might be soul, might be hot, sassy jazz. At some point, you'll probably move on to the chicken and port pâté with cornichons, or the plate of andouillette (herbed sausages). You'll look around in contented wonder and feast your eyes on the French bistro prints, the gas lamp hung with a metro sign, and the aproned, goateed waiters with plates on their forearms chattering away in unrecognizable French. You wonder if it could get any better, and you make a note to come back here as soon as you can. Ahh the French! Ahh the food! Ahh life! Entrées in the $13 range.

Financial District

Cafe Bastille, 22 Belden Place between Bush and Pine near Kearny; call (415) 986-5673 or fax (415) 986-1013. Open Monday–Saturday 11:30 A.M.–10:30 P.M.

69 / Been There, Done That, Now What?

Tours with a Difference

So, you've always wanted to jump out of a helicopter, eh? Believe it or not, you can do that or any number of other great things on one of the following special-interest tours. Prices vary according to when, where, and for how long.

Hunting Bargains offers five-hour personalized shopping tours of warehouses and designer outlets in the South of Market (SOMA) shopping district. You'll have to schlepp through endless aisles of merchandise but what's that compared to getting designer clothes for 20 to 75% off? (415) 892-1088.

Escape Artists Tours put you in touch with your wilder side. Hot air ballooning, air combat missions (*note:* author did not personally experience this tour), river rafting, cattle roundups, and spelunking (crawling into wet slimy caves). (800) 728-1384.

When you're done being wild, maybe you'd like a little luxury? Contact **European Limousine Tours**, which chauffeurs four to six passengers around town in stretch limousines with multilingual guides (German, Italian, Spanish, and French). (415) 221-9999.

Speaking of limos, call **Milieu** at (415) 673-7617 if you want to limo over to the studios of working artists and hang out with them as they go about the business of being "in people." Full- and half-day tours available.

How about a nice sedate day in the woods? **A Day in Nature** arranges for naturalist-led hikes through various Bay Area parks. Tour prices include lunch and pick-up. (415) 673-0548.

It's called saving the best for last: **3 Babes and a Bus Nightclub Tours**. Travel by luxury bus to four hot spots where you can instantly become part of the "in crowd." The $30 price includes transportation, all cover charges, and priority entry. Friday–Saturday, 9 P.M.–1:30 A.M. Reservations crucial. Call (415) 552-CLUB.

SOMA

70 / A Neighborhood of Nightclubs

Nightlife in SOMA

When it comes to nightlife, any San Franciscan will tell you to go south. South of Market, that is, or SOMA. So many clubs pack these streets, and the venues change so often that it's impossible to keep track. Here's a list of the best (which usually means they're also the most stable). Call before you go.

The **Up and Down Club**, 1151 Folsom, (415) 626-2388, is a hot spot part-owned by supermodel Christy Turlington. The hip crowd comes here for the live acid jazz on Mondays and on Wednesdays through Saturdays. Music usually starts at 9:30 P.M.; cover charge is $5 except on Wednesdays, when it's $3. Wednesday through Saturday, you can also get dinner from 7:30 P.M. to 10 P.M. Dancing upstairs.

Walking into the **Hotel Utah**, 500 Fourth Street at Bryant, (415) 421-8308, is like walking into your favorite jam-packed, twenty-something hang-out. There are three levels, 12 microbrews on tap, and not as much attitude as most other "hip" places. Downstairs has a live band and a dance floor. Open Monday through Friday 11:30 A.M.–2 A.M., Saturday 6 P.M.–2 A.M. and Sunday 5 P.M.–2 A.M. Upstairs there's an open mike night on Monday, acid jazz on Tuesday, and live music on Saturday with the bands varying from blues to alternative jazz to folk and country. Cover to $5, sometimes free.

The **Paradise Lounge**, 1501 Folsom at 11th, (415) 861-6906, has five bars, a pool room, three stages, and two levels. National and local bands perform mostly rock-type music to "in" people with attitude. Open Tuesday through Sunday 7 P.M.–2 A.M. The cover ranges from $3 to $7.

Boz Scaggs and Bob Brown, Huey Lewis's manager, opened a 600-seat venture in September 1988 and called it **Slim's** thinking it would be a strictly rhythm-and-blues club. Since then, the club has delved into the local alternative scene, world beat, jazz, rock, folk, and country. Slim's, (415) 621-3330, is at 333 11th Street between Folsom and Harrison.

SOMA

71 / An Arts Complex for All People
The Center for the Arts

It seems like just yesterday that this area was a maze of garbage-strewn lots and rundown houses. But today it's a $44-million museum and theater complex located above a subterranean portion of the Moscone Convention Center and dedicated to multicultural and experimental art. Its mainstays are the Ansel Adams Center for Photography, with an extraordinary collection of the great nature-photographer's work (yes, the Yosemite photographs are here, too); the Cartoon Art Museum, housing 11,000 original pieces, including syndicated newspaper strips, editorial and sports cartoons, original comic book pages and strips, and animation cels; the Jewish Museum, a wonderful collection of historical artifacts focusing on Jewish culture and tradition; and a number of galleries featuring current work by Bay Area residents. Future plans include building additional space for the Mexican Museum (now located at Fort Mason).

Don't leave without strolling through the area's outdoor spaces—the five-acre Yerba Buena Gardens urban park (see page 65) with fountains, statues, an outdoor performance area with lawn seating for 5,000, and enough flowers to qualify as a botanical garden. Especially wonderful is the walk-through waterfall memorial dedicated to Martin Luther King, Jr.

SOMA

The Center for the Arts, 701 Mission Street at Third; (415) 978-2787. Museums and galleries are open Tuesday–Sunday 11 A.M.–6 P.M. with extended hours until 9 P.M. on the first Thursday of each month. Admission charges: Ansel Adams Center for Photography, $4 adults, $2 youths 12–17; Cartoon Art Museum, $3.50 adults, $1.50 children.

72 / Thoroughly Modern

San Francisco Museum of Modern Art (SFMOMA)

In 1995, the year of its 60th anniversary, the West Coast's first modern art museum opened a striking new building that's worth a trip, even if you're one of those who views modern art as just a bunch of oversized canvases all painted black. The space, designed by Swiss architect Mario Botta, is a triumph—a 225,000-square-foot structure around a cavernous atrium, enormous sunlit galleries, and a 145-foot-tall skylight tower. Built at a cost of $60 million, the museum attracted a first-year attendance of 800,000, making it one of the top 10 most-visited museums in the country and one of San Francisco's top five tourist draws.

The collections are even more extraordinary than either the attendance figures or the architecture suggest. From Matisse to Frieda Kahlo, Stieglitz to Tina Modotti, Eames to Calder, SFMOMA's exhibits encompass photography, traditional painting and sculpture, design installations, and avant-garde multimedia exhibits—all located in 50,000-square feet of gallery space on four floors. There are also 200 well-trained docents on hand to provide public and private tours. A bookstore and very good cafe complete the picture; both are located on street level near the main entrance.

SOMA

San Francisco Museum of Modern Art (SFMOMA), 151 Third Street across from the Center for the Arts at Yerba Buena; (415) 357-4000, fax (415) 357-4037. Open Tuesday–Sunday 11 A.M.–6 P.M. with extended hours Thursday til 9 P.M. Admission is $7 adults, $3.50 children. First Tuesday of each month is free; Thursday 6 P.M.–9 P.M., half price.

73 / Climbing the Walls, Literally

Mission Cliffs Indoor Climbing Center

Successful travelers journey with maps, lists of sights-to-see, and good walking shoes. Successful travelers to San Francisco also get their muscles and tendons in shape for negotiating the vertical inclines that this city calls "streets." One great way to do this is to spend an afternoon or two on one of Mission Cliff's indoor climbing walls.

The Climbing Center is basically one big wall with a bunch of wedges stuck in at appropriate intervals. Naturally, the intervals are fewer and farther as one graduates to ever-more-advanced climbing levels. If you've never experienced indoor climbing, it's worth a trip just to see what it looks like—dozens (hundreds on evenings and weekends) of suited-up athletes (indoor climbing requires specific shoes and very elastic clothing) literally climbing the walls.

But if you're moved to do more than look, take a class. In one hour, you can learn everything you need to know about knot tying, belaying, and basic top-rope climbing. A Basic Technique class also puts you in the know about footwork, rest stances, body positioning, overhangs, and cracks.

The atmosphere is quiet, almost reverential, as befits a sport where one false move can send you tumbling into the abyss. Most people are members, but you can get a day pass for $12 ($9 under 14), and equipment rentals run $6 for a package that includes shoes, a harness, a chalk bag, and a belay device. Instruction is $23 for a basic safety package, $22 for a clinic, and $40 for a private lesson. After this, Telegraph Hill will look like an easy incline.

SOMA

Mission Cliffs Indoor Climbing Center, 2295 Harrison Street at 19th; (415) 550-0515, fax (415) 550-0524. Open Monday, Wednesday, and Friday 6:30 A.M.–10 P.M., Tuesday and Thursday 11 a.m.–10 p.m. and Saturday and Sunday 10 A.M.–6 P.M.

74 / A Lulu of a Restaurant
Lulu

When restaurateur Reed Hearon opened Lulu in 1993, he moved one step closer to becoming San Francisco's answer to Wolfgang Puck. Like Puck, Heron now has numerous restaurants to his name, award-winning cookbooks, and a line of food products all made at Lulu's and all absolutely sublime.

The menu he created for Lulu's was inspired by the foods of the Italian and French rivieras. The antipasti can be ordered individually or family style. Some of the best choices are the wood-oven-roasted whole portobello mushrooms with soft polenta, the seafood salad with potatoes, and the haricots verts with lemon and olive oil. A pizza will also do quite nicely as an appetizer—try the broccoli rabe pizza with pancetta and ricotta salata.

You're confronted with an entrée menu that will literally leave you reeling. Should you choose from the pasta menu, the wood-fired rotisserie menu, the grills and sautés, the shellfish platters? or the wood-fired oven menu? And that's not even to mention the excellent selection of vegetables (braised chard with pancetta and olive oil mashed potatoes are among the best). Lesser mortals have been felled by such challenges.

Rest assured, however, that whatever you choose, you will not be disappointed and that includes the exquisite desserts. From decor (the entire restaurant, kitchen included, is one huge, comfortable room whose focal point is a mammoth wood-burning oven and rotisserie) to service to the food—most especially the food—Lulu is one of San Francisco's best moderately priced restaurants (entrées in the $15 range).

SOMA

Lulu Restaurant, 816 Folsom Street between Fifth and Fourth; (415) 495-5775, fax (415) 495-7810. Open for lunch 11:30 A.M.–2:30 P.M. daily, dinner 5:30 P.M.–11 P.M. Sunday–Thursday, and 5 P.M.–12 A.M. Friday and Saturday. Reservations necessary.

75 / Facing the Wall
The Murals of the Mission

These murals are a part of history in the making; they are famous in Paris, Florence, Rome, and Tokyo; they are created by a resident community of artists, and—best of all—you won't find them in an ordinary San Francisco guidebook.

They are the murals of the Mission District. There are 200 of them, some as small as a garage door, and some as large as a three-story building. All are painted with brilliant colors and sometimes cause fender-benders and pedestrian collisions. Their messages are just as bold, ranging from the politics of nations to the preoccupations of the neighborhood. On a lucky day you can see a mural being created.

The murals lie largely in a 15-block area bounded on the west by Mission Street, on the east by Potrero, on the north by 20th Street and on the south by Precita Avenue (next to Precita Park). The greatest concentration lies in the 10 blocks from Mission to York on 24th Street. The Mission's art center, the Galeria de la Raza, stands at 24th Street and Bryant.

One of the more compelling murals lies at the southeast corner of the 24th Street BART station: Michael Rios's powerful evocation of the men who built BART. If you stand about midway on the south or uphill side of Precita Park, you'll get a stunning view of two other murals: one immediately across the park at the Leonard R. Flynn Elementary School, and one looming a block or so beyond in the Bernal Dwelling Housing Project.

The first community mural—actually a continuous string of 30 murals painted on garage doors and fences—is located on Balmy Alley off 24th Street. Nearby, at 348 Precita Avenue, you'll find the Precita Eyes Mural Center, which conducts Saturday mural tours. The tours are preceded by an informative and unpretentious slide show, that takes about two hours. For more information, call (415) 285-2287.

The Mission

76 / Burritoville

El Toro

The Mission District has dozens of Mexican restaurants, but none has more of a following than this unassuming little place on 17th Street. You can spot it when you're a few blocks away—it's the one with the line outside the door. But take heart, the line moves quickly in this casual place where you order at one end of the counter and find your tray ready and waiting when you sidle down to the cash register at the other end. Along the way, you get to watch the food being prepared: slabs of steak grilled to perfection over hot coals, vats of sublimely piquant salsa doused with fresh lime, and oversized tortillas steamed into submission. Everything is scrupulously clean and the restaurant is colorfully decorated with Mexican tiles, wooden tables, and leather-strung stools. There are three main choices: burritos, tacos, or quesadillas, and as you make your way along the line, you are asked to make a series of selections—meat or vegetarian, chicken, beef or pork, whole beans or refried, red or black, hot salsa or sweet. The faster you answer, the faster you get to the end of the line and get your food. Everything is cheap—unbelievably so (The Works Burrito: $4.95), and everything is served with crispy homemade tortilla chips. Drinks include a number of refreshing fruit beverages, beers, and sodas.

The Mission

El Toro, 598 Valencia at 17th; (415) 431-3351. Open daily 10 A.M.–10 P.M. No credit cards.

77 / Pay a Visit to San Francisco's Oldest Building

Mission Dolores

San Francisco got its start in 1776 (just five days before the signing of the Declaration of Independence) when Father Francisco Palou founded the sixth of California's missions along El Camino Real, the road linking Spanish missions from Mexico to Sonoma. Although the mission was officially named after St. Francis of Assisi, founder of the Franciscan Order, it soon became known as Mission Dolores because it was founded on the banks of the *Arroyo de los Dolores* (Stream of Sorrows).

The city's oldest structure, Mission Dolores has withstood four earthquakes and is the only one of the original 21 missions still in existence. An active parish, the small adobe chapel holds daily services at 7:30 A.M.

Mission Dolores's museum contains relics of the city's Spanish era as well as a number of very good colonial paintings. More than 5,000 Costanoan Indians are buried in the adjoining cemetery, whose garden is, nonetheless, a cheerful place with thousands of brilliant flowers.

When you're done viewing the historical part of the Mission, step into the adjoining Basilica, built in 1918 and christened by Pope Pius XII in 1952. Note the vaulted arches, the unusual domed ceiling, and the stained glass windows depicting the 21 missions whose founding led to the settlement of California.

The Mission

Mission Dolores, Dolores Street at 16th; (415) 621-8203. Open daily 9 A.M.–4:30 P.M. Admission is free although a donation is expected and appreciated.

78 / Country-Style Vietnamese Food

The Slanted Door

In 1973, Charles Phan migrated from Vietnam to San Francisco, where he worked as a busboy and waiter while attending the University of California at Berkeley. It was then that he realized how much he loved the restaurant business, but, as a technology graduate, he took up selling software. A few years ago, at 33, he finally decided to pursue his dream. His first thought was to open a street stall and sell Vietnamese crepes, but then he found the present location where he ultimately created this chic, sophisticated restaurant, whose stylish interior stands in perfect counterpoint to its honest, country-style food.

Most recipes are inspired by Phan's mother. The family is Chinese and the wonderful recipes tend to concentrate on Vietnamese food as created by the Chinese living in Vietnam. Among Phan's specialties are cool noodles topped with slices of hot ginger beef with scallions, bean sprouts, and julienne of ginger. His crepes are simple rice flour pancakes that emerge from the fryer hot and crispy and are immediately filled with cool bean sprouts, bits of pork, shrimp, and onions, served with a spicy fish sauce. The chicken curry is great—pie-shaped wedges of sweet potatoes, chunks of carrots, and chicken nuggets immersed in a coconut milk and curry sauce.

For dessert, try soursop and jackfruit ice cream or the flaky Napoleon with perfect blackberries sandwiched between puff pastry rounds. The wine list is small and exciting with 22 selections (including a Manzanilla sherry for those who know that nothing compliments Asian food better than dry sherry). Entrées range from $7 to $9.50, and there is often a line outside the door. Reservations for parties of six or more only.

The Mission

The Slanted Door, 584 Valencia Street near 17th; (415) 861-8032. Open Tuesday–Sunday 11:30 A.M.–10 P.M. Credit cards accepted.

79 / Happy Hour Havens

Where to Go for Free Food and Cheap Drinks

San Francisco used to be a great place to gather at the end of a day for $1 beers and platters of free buffalo wings. No more, but there are still a few places that do a great job preserving the ritual. Here are a few of the best.

The **Bottom of the Hill** has a mouthwatering Sunday tradition: from 4 P.M. to 8 P.M., $3 at the door lets you listen to an endless lineup of good bands while chomping on chicken, sausage, and pasta salads. Drinks are regular price, but this is such a great place that who cares? Friendly bartenders, cushy stools, and a well-maintained pool room await you at 2742 17th Street near Bryant; (415) 626-4455.

The noisy, lively, trendy **Cadillac Bar** offers probably the biggest spread in town, with platters of buffalo wings, beef and chicken chimichangas, tacos, corn fritters, nachos, tostadas, and chips and salsas. Their drink offer is pretty generous too—margaritas and well drinks are priced at a painless $2.75. The bar is at 325 Minna Street near 5th; (415) 543-8226. Happy hours are Monday through Friday 4 P.M.–6 P.M.

If you want to partake of your freebies surrounded by briefcase types, head to **Eddie Rickenbacker's**, which offers the most elegant of the after-work feeding frenzies. Spicy prawns, scallops, calamari, pâté, minipizzas, sweet-and-sour pork, etc. Food is free, but drinks are $3–$4. The bar is at 133 2nd Street, (415) 543-3498. Get happy Monday–Friday 5 P.M.–7 P.M.

The **Tonga Room**'s Happy Hour started out free a few years ago. But now it's $5 and a steal for an all-you-can-eat dim sum spread that includes pot stickers, shrimp dumplings, pork buns, barbecued pork, and cheese and fruit platters. There's a one-drink minimum with drinks running about $5, but the decor alone is worth the trip: Disneyland meets South Pacific complete with real tropical thundershowers that pour down around a pool. The Tonga Room Party is held at the Fairmont Hotel, 950 Mason Street at California; (415) 772-5278. Hours are Monday–Friday 5–7 P.M.

The Mission

80 / A Gay Place to Stay

24 Henry

The Castro is San Francisco's gay center; it's also where Rian Kelly and Walter Edgar, two transplanted southern Californians, decided in 1990, to open an intimate little guesthouse catering to anyone wanting to spend time in this wild and wacky part of town. A carefully and authentically restored 122-year-old Victorian, 24 Henry is located—where else—at 24 Henry Street, on a block filled with other Victorians lucky enough to have survived the fires accompanying the 1906 earthquake. The guesthouse boasts five large distinctively decorated rooms with extra-high ceilings and private answering machines. A delicious continental buffet breakfast is served in both the front and back parlors of the first floor; Rian and Walter make many of the pastries themselves.

Four of 24 Henry's five rooms share a large double shower room and separate water closet. The master bedroom has its own bath, and is located at the back of the house, overlooking the garden and patio, where you can plop down after a frenetic day of sightseeing and just relax. Public transportation is convenient and close by—there's great access to all five MUNI Metro lines and the historic "F" line. Everyone is welcome, but there is no smoking allowed in any of the rooms.

The Castro

---

24 Henry, 24 Henry Street in the Castro District; (415) 864-5686 or (800) 900-5686, fax (415) 864-0406. Rates range from $55 for a single room to $90 for the master bedroom.

81 / No Name Is a Good Name
The Restaurant at 2223 Market Street

For some reason, owner John Cunin just never got around to naming this Castro hotspot. He even ran a contest offering to pay $1,000 for a winning moniker that 2,000 people entered, but it's quickly becoming clear that both Cunin and his clientele like the anonymity. Not that it prevents people from coming, mind you. One visit and you'll know why.

The food is hip, fresh, imaginative, and unpretentious. The same for the wine list. And it's refreshing to meet waiters who actually look like they're glad you came. Try a cocktail before you bury your nose in the menu—maybe a 2223 Negroni made with gin, campari, sweet vermouth, and a splash of orange juice.

But do get to the food, which is basic California cuisine given a new twist by Chef Melinda Randolph. The small excellent menu changes daily, but there are generally five appetizers, four pizzas, eight entrées (one vegetarian), and five desserts. Start with one of the standards: the pancetta pizza with creamy Teleme cheese, shards of pancetta, and sweet caramelized onions. Another excellent standard is the smoked salmon salad, which is as beautiful as it is good (spikes of flatbread topped with salmon and splayed out on a dark blue plate to resemble a starfish). Entrées include roasted chicken with a whirlwind of fried onion rings and rustic beef stew served in puff pastry on a bed of carrots and pearl onions.

Appetizers run from $6 to $9; entrées from $9 to $16. There are 27 tables, and although the restaurant does take reservations, they like to leave half of the space for walk-ins. The crowd is trendy, largely gay, and very spirited.

The Castro

The Restaurant at 2223 Market Street, 2223 Market Street at Sanchez; (415) 431-0692. Open for lunch 11:30 A.M.–2:30 P.M. Monday–Friday, Dinner 5:30 P.M.–10 P.M. Sunday–Thursday and till 11 P.M. on Saturday and Sunday. Brunch is served 10 A.M.–2 P.M. on Sunday. The bar is open from 11:00 A.M. to closing Monday through Friday, from 5:00 P.M. to closing on Saturday, and from 10:00 A.M. to closing on Sunday.

82 / Memories from the Summer of Love

A Short Musical Memory Tour Through the Haight

When Jerry Garcia died on August 9, 1995, Haight-Ashbury flashed right back to the '60s as Deadheads gathered by the thousands in rainbow tie-dye to remember their guitarist guru. Streams of devoted fans made their way to the house at 710 Ashbury Street where Garcia and the Grateful Dead lived during the heyday of the hippie era. The word *hippie* came from ex-*San Francisco Examiner* writer Michael Fallon who coined it as a way to differentiate this hip new group from the beatniks. In fact, it was just down the street from this three-story Victorian, known as Haight-Ashbury's unofficial City Hall, where in October 1968, after the Dead had achieved fame and fortune, the band played an informal gig from a flatbed truck parked in the middle of Haight Street. The concert was a farewell gesture to the neighborhood before the Dead moved to Marin County, just north of the Golden Gate Bridge.

Just blocks away, the monstrous four-story mansion at 2400 Fulton Street became the home, office, rehearsal hall, and party haven for the Jefferson Airplane in 1968. The facade at the time was painted black and the house, known as the "Airplane Mansion" served as a kind of underground landmark.

Janis Joplin also lived nearby, at 112 Lyon Street, when she and her band, Big Brother and the Holding Company, first struck it big at the 1967 Monterey Pop Festival. And at 42 Belvedere Street, ballet dancers Rudolf Nureyev and Margot Fonteyn were arrested for smoking pot at a 1967 party.

Some of these people are gone now, but a stroll through the Haight will serve to bring back their memories as well as provide you with a fun time immersing yourself in the still very-much-happenin' hippie spirit.

Haight-Ashbury

83 / You Just Knew There Had to Be a Place Like This

Red Victorian Peace Center B&B

Forget the Hilton! For a true San Francisco experience—albeit one skewed toward a '60s style—check into this one-of-a-kind overnight adventure. Scrupulously clean, amazingly inexpensive, and as alternative as a bed-and-breakfast could possibly get, a stay at the Red Vic will truly be something to write home about.

Its actual name is the Red Victorian Peace Center B&B; that's because there's a meditation room, a host of meditation tapes you can borrow to take to bed, a Gallery of Meditative Art, and a resident "insight counselor," Cheryl Canfield, with whom you can book a one-on-one session.

But the best part is the series of rooms—18 of them, all beautifully decorated in a peerlessly distinctive style. You can choose from the Flower Child, which has rainbows, clouds, roses, and a sun painted on the ceiling and '60s posters on the walls. Or the Playground Room, with a ceiling canopy and walls emblazoned with authentic carousel posters celebrating the country's first public playground erected in nearby Golden Gate Park. Or even the Teddy Bear Room, filled to overflowing with teddy bears and maps. For those with a bit more to spend, there's the Peacock Suite, with an exotically canopied king-size bed, stained glass windows, and a private bath with the a moon window.

Four of the 18 rooms have a private bath; the others have private sinks but share the Love, Aquarium, Starlight, or Infinity bathrooms. Rates range from $76 to $120 per day per couple and $200 for the Peacock Suite. All prices include a family-style buffet breakfast.

Haight-Ashbury

The **Red Victorian Peace Center B&B**, 1665 Haight Street near Cole; (415) 864-1978.

84 / California Dreamin'

Beaches

If you're craving bikinis and the smell of suntan oil, go south. Northern California is different from the south in almost every aspect, but none more striking than in their respective beach cultures. The weather and water here are colder—much colder. But oh, those views and the sounds of sea lions!

Ocean Beach lies along the western end of the city and features four miles of sandy shoreline. At least once a day during tourist season an unsuspecting novice goes running into the frigid waves only to rigidify upon contact. At the beach's northern end, you can spot what's commonly known as "Seal Rock" (it's the one lathered with 14 tons of guano). Actually, you'll probably hear the seals before you see the rock. Also at the northern end is the historic Cliff House Restaurant, sitting majestically on a bluff above the shore. It's a good place to go at day's end for a glass of wine. Ocean Beach is often fogged in, but definitely worth a trip when it's not.

Tucked away behind the million-dollar homes of the Seacliff district (Robin Williams lives here) is **China Beach**, one of the city's few beaches safe for swimming. Lifeguards are on duty during the summer, and there are changing rooms, barbecue pits, and an enclosed sundeck. A good place for kids, China Beach is accessible from Seacliff and 28th Avenue, near El Camino del Mar. After a chilly swim (summer water temperatures hover in the 60s), a game of Frisbee is a great way to warm up.

Baker Beach stretches along the western shore of the Presidio below Lincoln Boulevard. Although swimming is dangerous because of swift currents, hikers and sunbathers are treated to the ubiquitous sound of sea lions and to gorgeous views of the Golden Gate Bridge and the Marin Headlands. You reach the beach via a long stairway down naturally landscaped cliffs, and the panoramic view of blue sky and verdant hillside is truly spectacular. *A word to the modest:* nude sunbathing is the rule at this beach's northern end.

Golden Gate

85 / The Next Best Thing to Walking on Water

A Walk Across the Golden Gate Bridge

Author Susan Cheever compares it to the towers of Paris's Chartres Cathedral. Mikhail Gorbachev said it reminded him of a lithesome ballet dancer stretching out her arms and legs in "one unbroken elegant reach." Tony Bennett says, well, we all know what Tony Bennett says. The Golden Gate is the world's most celebrated bridge. Built in 1937 to reflect the era's opulent Art Deco taste, it has since inspired hordes of poets and pundits attracted by its perfect blend of architecture and nature. There may be longer, taller, more intricate spans, but there is none more beautiful, with spectacular coastlines on both sides, the Marin Headlands on the north, and a gorgeous city sparkling like a jewel to the south. Furthermore, what kind of machine would be necessary to create the great billowy banks of fog quintessential to its charms?

Drive across it, but understand that there is no better way to appreciate the Golden Gate than by walking its 1.7 mile length. Park at one of the lots and walk out as far as is necessary to feel the sway and get that amazing unobstructed view of Alcatraz, Angel Island, the city skyline, and an endless parade of sailboats, windsurfers, and freighters.

Choose your time: when it's clear and sunny, the reward lies in what you can see; and when it's foggy, in the romantic fact that you can't see as much. Either way, it will be one of the highlights of your trip and well worthwhile. Dress warmly—it'll be cold no matter when you go. There are free parking lots on both sides of the bridge; weekdays are better than weekends when spots tend to fill up by noon.

Golden Gate

86 / Culture in the Park

The M. H. de Young Memorial and Asian Art Museums

In 1893 M. H. de Young, publisher of the *San Francisco Chronicle*, decided that the West was in need of a World's Fair and by January 29, 1894, the California Midwinter International Exposition opened in Golden Gate Park. When the fair closed, de Young pushed to establish a permanent museum in the park as a memorial to the exposition. The new museum opened its doors on March 24, 1895, and was an instant success.

With paintings by Whistler, Sargent, Wood, Eakins, Cassatt, and O'Keeffe as well as sculptures, pre-Columbian art, African art, and a wonderful textile collection, the de Young contains one of California's foremost collections.

The Asian Art Museum shares the de Young's home, but will move to the old city library building by the year 2000. With a permanent collection containing more than 12,000 objects from over 40 Asian countries including India, Thailand, Vietnam, and Korea, it is the world's largest collection of Asian art outside Asia, which makes sense since San Francisco is home to the world's largest Asian population outside Asia itself. The Chinese collection alone is worth a visit, with more than 4,000 items spanning 60 centuries. The Asian's range of items is truly impressive, with paintings, bronzes, jades, porcelains, and textiles as well as amazing statues and—for the military enthusiast—samurai armor, Japanese swords, and Korean war relics.

Golden Gate

The M. H. de Young Memorial and **Asian Art Museums** are located on the Music Concourse in Golden Gate Park; (415) 668-8921. Exhibition hotline: (415) 863-3330. Open Wednesday–Sunday 10:00 A.M.–4:45 P.M.; open until 8:45 P.M. on Wednesday. There is one admission for both museums: $6 adults, $3 children under 12. Admission free on the first Wednesday of each month.

87 / Eyeball to Eyeball with a Barracuda

The California Academy of Sciences

Board "The Safe Quake" and experience a simulated earthquake. Take a deep sea dive without getting wet in a 100,000 gallon circular tank. Journey back 3.5 billion years and say hello to life-size dinosaurs and giant insects.

Welcome to "The Academy," a huge education and research institute that is really three museums under one roof: the Steinhart Aquarium, the Morrison Planetarium, and the San Francisco Natural History Museum. The aquarium has everything you'd expect including an amazing wrap-around fish tank (The Fish Roundabout), ingeniously designed to allow you to stand still as sandsharks and barracudas race by. It also has a hilarious colony of frolicking penguins that are fed twice daily by adoring employees.

The planetarium is a 309-seat theater whose giant gas laser projects luminous stars onto a 65-foot perforated dome and makes you feel like you're hurtling through outer space. Approximately 3,800 stars shine above your head while you sit back and listen to stories about galaxies, black holes, and the earth's solar system delivered against a backdrop of music ranging from classical to rock.

The museum contains everything from an insect room and a snake area to a gem and mineral hall. But your kids' favorite space will undoubtedly be the Discovery Room, a hands-on-everything place loaded with touchable specimens of bones, sea shells, fossils, and even the dried skin of a spiny porcupine fish.

Golden Gate

The California Academy of Sciences, Golden Gate Park; (415) 750-7145. Open seven days a week 10 A.M.–5 P.M. with extended hours until 7:00 P.M. July 4th through Labor Day. General admission: $7 for adults, $4 for youths (12–17), $1.50 for children 6–11, and free for children 5 and under. Planetarium admission is an extra $2.50 for adults and $1.25 for those 17 and under.

88 / Pagodas, Buddhas, and Afternoon Tea

The Japanese Tea Garden

Why travel all the way to Japan when you can experience the next best thing in Golden Gate Park's Japanese Tea Garden? Planted originally by George Turner Marsh as part of the 1894, California Midwinter International Exposition and enlarged with gardens donated in 1953 by a number of Japanese cities, the tea garden is the most elegant five acres in the park. With Shinto pagodas, quiet garden paths, arched bridges, koi-filled ponds, strategically placed stones, and an enormous statue of the Buddha towering over its surroundings, the garden is a perfect evocation of old world Japan.

There are visitors—busloads of them on any given day. But it still is worth a trip, if only for the meditative value of a simple half hour spent walking alongside serene ponds. The tea pagoda serves steaming pots of Japanese tea and fortune cookies to contented guests placidly gazing out over stands of magenta-colored rhododendrons and white cherry blossoms. Long ago, the cookie baking and tea service was carried out by a Japanese family who lived on the grounds. But when the War Department exiled San Francisco's Japanese population during the World War II, the task was assumed by Australians. Today, reason has been restored and the teahouse is once again run by Japanese hosts. The Buddha, by the way, was cast in 1790 in Tajima-ken, Japan, and is the largest Buddha ever imported by the U.S. It was a gift to the park in 1949 from Gump's department store.

Golden Gate

The Japanese Tea Garden, Tea Garden Drive in Golden Gate Park; (415) 666-7100. Open daily 10 A.M.–5 P.M. Adults: $2; children 6–12, $1.

89 / Where Pebble Beach Meets Ocean Beach

Golf Courses

The world's most famous golf courses are known as much for their gorgeous settings as they are for their levels of difficulty. San Francisco has not one, but two golf courses as beautiful as any with the added attraction that you don't have to pay thousands of dollars to play. The first is Lincoln Park Golf Course where you can swing against a backdrop that is truly magnificent. Its tees have views of the ocean and the Golden Gate, and its fairways are lined with venerable redwood and cypress trees. The impeccably maintained course is rated at par 68, and there is rarely a waiting line. Greens fees are $21 on weekdays; $25 on weekends. Club rentals are $10 and golf carts, $20.

The other option, Golden Gate Course, is only nine holes, but its location—two drives and a chip shot from Ocean Beach—makes it an extremely desirable destination for golfers who want to make golfing part of an all-day excursion to Golden Gate Park. A par 27 course, Golden Gate charges $8 weekdays; $11 on weekends.

Golden Gate

Lincoln Park Golf Course, 34th Avenue & Clement near the California Palace of the Legion of Honor; (415) 221-9911.

Golden Gate Golf Course, 47th Avenue & Fulton; (415) 221-9911.

90 / Paris on the Pacific
The California Palace of the Legion of Honor

It was closed in 1992 for seismic retrofitting and general renovation. But now it's back—the "Elegant Lady Poised on the Hill," as the California Palace of the Legion of Honor is known by its adoring fans. One of the most striking museum buildings in the world, the palace was modeled after Paris's Palais de la Legion d'Honneur. Built to "honor the dead while serving the living," it was dedicated to the memory of the 3,600 Californians who died during World War I and opened on Armistice Day, November 11, 1924.

The museum houses 4,000 years of ancient and European art, including works by El Greco, Rubens, Rembrandt, Steen, Van Gogh, Monet, Matisse, Whistler, Audubon, Degas, and Toulouse-Lautrec. The Assyrian wall relief ranks as one of ancient Mesopotamia's finest achievements.

The museum is also home to one of the country's leading collections of bronze sculptures by Auguste Rodin (*The Thinker* is here), as well as a newly restored 15th-century Spanish ceiling, extensive holdings of 17th- through 19th-century porcelains, and three period rooms. Out in front, across the road, you'll find George Segal's sculpture, *The Holocaust*, recalling the World War II European horror.

The museum's interior is as much an art object as any piece in its collections, from the Tennessee Pink marble floors, Napoleon Grey marble columns, and the ornate plaster cornices to the Italian-style faux marble finish that covers the walls of the stairwells and hallways. On the lower level, the special 9,500-square-foot temporary exhibition gallery is divided into six rooms organized around a central, beautifully skylit courtyard.

Golden Gate

The California Palace of the Legion of Honor, Lincoln Park, 34th Avenue & Clement; (415) 863-3330. Open Tuesday–Sunday, 10 A.M.–5 P.M. with extended hours on the first Saturday of each month until 8:45 P.M. Admission: $6 adults, $3 youths 12–17, free for children under 12. Admission is free the second Wednesday of every month.

91 / A Big, Beautiful Backyard

Golden Gate Park

It's hard to believe that 125 years ago, lush 1,017-acre Golden Gate Park was a barren stretch of sand dunes. In fact, when William Hammond Hall began the reclamation project in 1870, San Francisco didn't even extend to the park's borders. Scottish landscape gardener John McLaren stabilized the dunes with scores of cypress, pine, and eucalyptus trees. Today, 4,000 tree species thrive in the park.

On a sunny day, the park is filled with joggers, strollers, roller-bladers, and cyclists. Its splendid gardens include the 70-acre Strybing Arboretum and Botanical Gardens, with over 6,000 plant species, a Fragrance Garden, a Japanese Moon-Viewing Garden, and a sunny lake filled with mallards. The park is also home to three world-class museums (see page 87), a buffalo paddock, a trendy in-line skating dance area, and a number of lakes, among them Stow Lake, where you can rent rowboats and while away the afternoon. Park maps are available at McLaren Lodge at the Fell Street entrance.

Following is a summary of things to do in the park and numbers to call for information or rentals: horseback riding lessons and horse rentals (415) 668-7360; tennis court reservations (415) 753-7100 and tennis lessons (415) 681-0130. Bicycle and roller-blade rentals can be arranged in any of the numerous places on and around Haight Street. Guided walks take place weekends May through October. There are six separate tours. For dates, times, and information, call (415) 221-1311. Free lawn bowling lessons are available at the bowling greens south of the tennis courts (415) 753-9298.

Golden Gate

Golden Gate Park is bordered by Stanyan Street, the Great Highway, Lincoln Way and Fulton Street. For information, call (415) 666-7200 8 A.M.–5 P.M. on weekdays.

92 / Animal House

The San Francisco Zoo

If you like koalas (and who doesn't like koalas?), a trip to the San Francisco Zoo is a must. You might, in fact, want to head right for their home base, called Koala Crossing, and just spend the day. Pick a sunny day though—koalas love sun as much as we do. Equally cute is the Children's Zoo, right near the front entrance, where you can pet farm animals, peer at creepy-crawlies in the big indoor Insect Zoo, and go for a ride on a restored antique carousel.

Other don't-miss areas include Gorilla World (where there might be some newborns), Penguin Island with its lively colony of Magellanic penguins and their fledglings, Otter River, and the Discovery Center, where 15 species of rare and endangered monkeys live and play in a spectacular series of bi-level glass vaults. A visit to the Lion House will yield a view of Prince Charles, the zoo's rare white Bengal tiger. Further along the trail, just beyond the sea lions, you'll find the classic bear pits modeled after the famous Hagenbeck Zoo in Germany. The pits house numerous types of bears, including polar bears and brown bears.

When you've walked up a good appetite, amble over to the Terrace Cafe, which serves ethnic food and gourmet sandwiches; or the Plaza Cafe, where you can get pizza, fried wontons, Polish sausages, and—because this is California—cappuccino.

Lake Merced

The San Francisco Zoo, Sloat Boulevard at 44th Avenue; (415) 753-7080. Open daily 10 A.M.–5 P.M. Admission: $6.50 adults, $3 ages 12–15, $1 ages 6–11. The Children's Zoo is open daily 11 A.M.–4 P.M. and requires an additional $1 for admission.

93 / Go Tell It on the Mountain
Mount Tamalpais State Park

Don't call it Mount Tamalpais if you don't want to be instantly branded as a tourist. It's Mount Tam, spoken with an offhand jauntiness that certifies the cool insider way in which you—like all other San Franciscans—express your absolute adoration of this mountain. Part of a 6,220-acre nature preserve established in 1927, Tam is everybody's mountain. Hikers, mountain bikers, runners, horseback riders, fishers, photographers, picnickers— even thespians, who flock to its Summer Mountain Theater to sit on the 4,000 stones of the open-air amphitheater laid out in the 1930s by the ccc.

Tam's highest point is no big deal—a mere 2,571 feet. In fact, it's arguably not even a mountain. It's more of a ridge trending east to west. But it encompasses everything from grassy knolls to oak woodlands, redwood forests, steep canyons, virginal falls, wildflowers, lakes and, of course, the ubiquitous mule deer. In fact, the display of nature is so abundant and pristine that it's hard to believe you're only 15 miles from San Francisco.

There's only one problem: Mt. Tam is located off of the same road that everything else north of the city is located along— Highway 1—and it generally crawls with traffic on weekends; not to mention that parking can be an Excedrin headache. So go during the week, or if you do go on weekends, leave early and park in one of the larger lots at Rock Springs or Lagunitas Lake. You can also take Golden Gate Transit bus 63 from the Golden Gate Bridge. For bus schedule, call (415) 923-2000.

Out of Town

Mount Tamalpais State Park is located in Marin County. For detailed directions, call (415) 388-2070.

94 / Merrily We Roll Along
The Napa Valley Wine Train

You're sitting comfortably in an ornate parlor car, sipping wine and listening to soft music, a tuxedoed staff at your beck and call. The soothing rhythms of a train sound beneath you, and the view outside your window is of consistently gorgeous countryside. No, you're not on the Orient Express. You're on board the Napa Valley Wine Train, and, right about now, you're probably thinking to yourself, life doesn't get any better than this.

Reminiscent of old time luxury rail travel, the Napa Valley Wine Train journeys 36 miles past 26 wineries between Napa and St. Helena. Dining options include brunch, lunch, dinner, or a deli meal; all are prepared on the train itself and served on white linen aboard elegantly refurbished 1915-vintage Pullman coaches, replete with swivel lounge chairs, comfy love seats, rich polished woods, etched glass, plush carpeting, and upholstered walls. There's even a tea rose in a pewter vase to grace your table.

The wine list is extensive and impressive, and, as a grand finale, you're served dessert and cordials in a lounge car ornamented with hand-rubbed mahogany and polished brass trim. You can dress casually for brunch and lunch, but there is a dress code for dinner rides—jackets and ties.

Travel time is three hours and there's no stopping at any of the wineries, but winery touring is not the point here. More a culinary experience than a sightseeing trip, the Wine Train is a great way to get the feel of wine country without lining up on traffic-clogged highways.

Out of Town

The Napa Valley Wine Train leaves from 1275 McKinstry Street in Napa, an hour's drive north of San Francisco. Brunch or lunch trips: $52–55 per person, dinner: $64. Wine extra. Call (800) 427-4124.

95 / A Very Fishy Place
The Monterey Bay Aquarium

It's called "The Nation's Best Aquarium," and after spending a few hours here, you'll wonder why they didn't just go ahead and claim "universal" besthood. Not only does it have many, many species, but it houses them all in absolutely astonishing environments. The million-gallon indoor ocean is viewed through an enormous window that let's you see sleek speedy tuna, ocean sunfish that weigh more than a ton each, sea turtles, barracuda, and enormous sharks. The Outer Bay gallery puts you in the world of the open ocean: the bat ray petting pool, the two-story sea otter tank where you can see the little critters even when they plummet down to the bottom, the towering three-story living kelp forest, and the unique jelly fish gallery.

More than a hundred galleries and exhibits recreate the bay's many habitats, from shallow tide pools to the vast open ocean located just outside the facility. The aquarium has also ingeniously installed a number of telescopes and microscopes for those wanting a closer inspection of the underwater worlds. You can, for example, witness the dancing plankton and other miniature sea creatures cavorting in their invisible environments or watch sea otters as they wiggle through the offshore kelp beds.

The Monterey Aquarium is 110 miles south of San Francisco off Highway 1 and can be reached by car or Greyhound Bus.

Out of Town

The Monterey Bay Aquarium, 886 Cannery Row, Monterey; (408) 648-4860. Admission: $13.75 adult; $11.75 students 13–17 with ID; $6 children 3–12.

96 / Italy Across the Bay

Oliveto's

Paul Bertolli is a chef who likes to get his hands into everything. That's why he starts many of his days with a visit to San Francisco's Farmers Market where he can cruise the stalls and pick the freshest seasonal ingredients. His theory of running a restaurant is somewhat contrary to that of most other people: He decides what to cook after he's looked at what's good that day. If it's the height of string bean season, you can count on finding more than one menu item encompassing those slender stalks of green. "To make a menu, you have to be entirely open," he says. "You have to be in tune with what's going on seasonally, excited by what you have in front of you and not predisposed to choose any particular thing. Cooking is a responsive act."

As a result of this spontaneity, Bertolli is widely acknowledged as one of America's best chefs and Oliveto's as an absolute must for anyone traveling to the Bay area. So noted is this Chez Panisse graduate (10 years as head chef) in fact, that his regular customers simply wave aside the menu and ask him to cook them a meal.

The menu at Oliveto's changes constantly, but count on eating like you've never eaten before regardless of when you go. For one thing, Bertolli and his staff make as much as they can themselves: pasta, prosciutto, bread—a few years ago, Paul even started making his own balsamic vinegar and the first elixers should be just about ready. A large breezy restaurant located directly across the street from the Rock Ridge BART, Oliveto's interior is as satisfying as its food. Entrées are in the $15 range.

Out of Town

Oliveto's 5655 College Avenue, Oakland; (510) 547-5356. Lunch and dinner Tuesday–Sunday. Major credit cards accepted.

97 / The Tallest Trees in the World

Muir Woods Redwood Park

Actually you won't find the tallest redwoods here—those are a little farther up the California coast. But with trees reaching upward of 250 feet, Muir Woods will nonetheless leave you utterly enchanted. Located just 12 miles north of the Golden Gate Bridge, magnificent Muir Woods is part of Mount Tamalpais State Park (see page 93). Packed with giant virgin redwoods, some more than 1,000 years old, the park can be both incredibly crowded and serenely silent depending how far you want to walk. The wood-paved trail that lies within one mile of the parking lot throngs with tourists (especially on weekends and in Bohemian Grove and Cathedral Grove which are parts of the half-mile loop containing the park's tallest trees). Journey just a wee bit farther, however, along the unpaved trails that lead up out of the canyon, and—especially on a weekday—you probably won't meet another soul. Either way, you'll achieve more than a passing acquaintance with these majestic giants. You'll also experience a profound sense of relaxation as you stroll along paths lined with ferns and azaleas and scented with the fragrance of deep woods. Remember, however, that you'll be in the woods, and no matter how sunny it is, bring a jacket. To reach Muir Woods, take U.S. Highway 101 to Highway 1, then the Panoramic Highway to Muir Woods Road.

Out of Town

Muir Woods, Redwood Park, Muir Woods Road, Mill Valley; (415) 388-2595. Open daily 8 A.M.–sunset. Admission is free.

98 / Orca by the Bay

Marine World Africa USA

Kids won't need any motivating to go to this wildlife theme park 35 miles north of the city. For that matter, neither will most adults. Suffice to say there's a spectacular killer whale and dolphin show with animals jumping high into the air, whizzing through the holding tank in perfect rhythm, and even kissing willing child volunteers. *A word to the wise:* Don't sit in the first few rows unless it's really sunny, and you're aching for a good soaking.

Marine World's stated intent is to "educate as well as entertain" so the animals are spared having to perform silly tricks. As a result, there's less time spent staring at them in isolated environments and more opportunities to actually move through their indigenous worlds. In the Shark Experience, for example, you climb onto a ramp that moves right through the middle of an enormous shark tank. In the Prairie Crawl, kids scramble through tunnels then pop up into glassed-in stalls for up-close views of prairie dogs. There are also two theme playgrounds, Whale of a Time and Bill's Backyard, where kids can assume animal identities and run off some steam.

Marine World also offers the Tiger and Lion Show (the cats here provided the voices for *Jurassic Park*), the Incredible Acrobats of China, and a Water-Skiing Show. You can also watch the tigers devour their food at Tiger Island, ride an elephant (for an extra $3), and feed a giraffe. It's a great way to learn about the natural world while having an enormous amount of fun.

Marine World can be reached via ferry (both Blue & Gold and Red & White lines have package trips), Gray Line Bus, or by car.

Out of Town

Marine World Africa USA, Marine World Parkway, Vallejo; (707) 643-6722. Open Memorial Day–Labor Day as well as Easter Week, Spring Break Week, and December 26–January 1. Wednesday–Sunday, 9:30 A.M.–dusk. Admission: $24.95 adults, $17.95 for children 4–12.

99 / Subversively Educational
The Bay Area Discovery Museum

Don't tell the kids you're going to another museum—believe me, they'll never figure out that's what it is. The Discovery Museum offers hundreds of interactive exhibits and classes—all are geared to what they call "Learning Through Play." On the life-size fishing boat for example, children chart a course, operate the compass, and learn to tie knots and drop fishing nets. They can also crawl through the Underwater Sea Tunnel that runs beneath the boat. At the construction site, they can put on hard hats and use hand-operated cranes to learn about the inner workings of high-rise buildings. In the Space Maze, they can turn their drawings into 3-D images.

There are five exhibit halls: the Science Lab, the Media Center, the Transportation Exhibit, the Maze of Illusions, and an exhibit that changes periodically. The museum also recently added a number of exhibits designed to attract teenagers. Yesterday, Today, and Tomorrow, for example, lets kids use computers to solve traffic snarls. Outside the museum there's a sculpture garden created entirely by kids, and, of course, there's the ever-present view of magnificent San Francisco Bay.

The Bay Area Discovery Museum is in Sausalito and can be reached by car via the Golden Gate Bridge, or by ferry—take the Red & White Fleet from Fisherman's Wharf (415) 546-2628; round trip adult, $11; children, $5.50.

Out of Town

The Bay Area Discovery Museum, 557 E. Fort Baker Road at Murray Circle, Sausalito; (415) 487-4398. Open Wednesday–Sunday 10 A.M.–5 P.M. Admission: $5.

100 / Luscious Country

Napa and Sonoma Valleys

Just 50 miles north of San Francisco, Napa is only a tinge more famous than its sister valley, Sonoma, but the two are dead equal in their ability to consistently turn out world-class wines. Sonoma is considered to have ideal conditions for chardonnay and pinot noir.

Napa Valley lies west of Sonoma. Over 35 miles in length, it is home to over 150 wineries, most of which line the ever-crowded Highway 29. Some wineries charge for tasting; others simply sell the wine without any presampling.

Here are a few wineries that you might try:

Napa   Beaulieu, Rutherford (707) 963-2411; Beringer, St. Helena (707) 963-4812; Charles Krug, St. Helena (707) 963-5057; Cosentino, Yountville (707) 944-1220; Conn Creek, St. Helena (707) 963-9100; Domaine Chandon, Yountville (707) 944-2280; Hakusan Sake Gardens, Napa (707) 258-6160; Inglenook, Rutherford (707) 967-3363; Kornell Larkmead, Calistoga (707) 942-0859; Robert Mondavi, Oakville (707) 963-9611; Mumm Napa Valley, Rutherford (707) 942-3434; Sterling, Calistoga (707) 942-3344; Sutter Home, St. Helena (707) 963-3104

Sonoma   Buena Vista, Sonoma (707) 938-1266; Clos du Bois, Healdsburg (707) 433-5576; Ferrari-Carano, Healdsburg (707) 433-6700; Glen Ellen, Glen Ellen (707) 935-4046; Kenwood, Kenwood (707) 833-5891; Korbel Champagne, Guerneville (707) 887-2294; Piper Sonoma, Healdsburg (707) 433-8843; Ravenswood, Sonoma (707) 938-1960; Sebastiani, Sonoma (707) 938-5532; Simi, Healdsburg (707) 433-6981

Out of Town

101 / Hot Jazz on the Other Side of the Bay

Yoshi's Restaurant and Jazz Club

When Yoshi Aikiba and Kaz Kajimura first opened this place, it was strictly a restaurant serving luscious Japanese food. It's still a restaurant serving luscious Japanese food, but the food has long since been eclipsed by the music. And what music it is. World-class jazz performers strut their stuff 365 days a year in a state-of-the-acoustical-art roomy paradise where every person has a good view and enough room to sway and groove to their hearts' content.

Check out Yoshi's lobby if you want to see what kind of talent they get here—wall-to-wall photos of the best in the business—Roy Hargrove, Kenny Barron, the Modern Jazz Quartet, Milt Hinton, Joe Sample. Mondays and Tuesdays are reserved for local talent, which, in this town, means something slightly different than it does in, say, Peoria. Ticket prices on those nights range from $6 to $8. The rest of the week is devoted to national luminaries who cost somewhat more to experience, usually from $15 to $20. Performances are always at 8 P.M. and 10 P.M.

Because there's open seating, doors open at 6 P.M. for 8:00 P.M. performances. But you don't have to wait for two hours to get the seat of your choice. The manager will give you a yellow sticker that you simply place on the back of your chosen seat. That's it. Now you can go to dinner wherever you want (Yoshi's is the best choice) and just be back by 8 P.M. Very smart!

To get to Yoshi's, take the ferry to Oakland's Jack London Square or take the BART to the 12th Street Oakland stop.

Out of Town

Yoshi's Restaurant and Jazz Club, 6030 Claremont Avenue, Oakland; (510) 652-9200. Open daily 5 P.M. until the end of the last show.

Index

A

Academy Grill, 36
Act IV (restaurant), 39
Alamo Square, 52
Albona, 49
Alcatraz, 1
Angel Island, 3
Ansel Adams Center for Photography, 71
Aqua (restaurant), 64
Archbishop's Mansion (hotel), 20
Asian Art Museum, 86

B

Baker Beach, 84
Bars and nightclubs
  Biscuits 'n' Blues, 17
  Bottom of the Hill, 79
  Cadillac Bar, 79
  Cafe du Nord, 43
  Club Fugazi, 45
  Coconut Grove, 43
  DNA Lounge, 43
  Fillmore, the, 18
  Finocchio's, 35
  Hi-Ball Lounge, 43
  Hotel Utah, 70
  New Orleans Room, 33, 35
  Paradise Lounge, 70
  Plush Room, 35
  Rasselas, 17
  San Francisco Brewing Company, 41
  Slim's, 70
  Tonga Restaurant and Hurricane Bar, 33, 79
  Up and Down Club, 70
  Yoshi's Restaurant and Jazz Club, 101
Bay Area Discovery Museum, 99
Bay-to-Breakers Race, 26
Bay View Cafe, 23
Beach Blanket Babylon (show), 45
Beaches
  Baker Beach, 84
  China Beach, 84
  Ocean Beach, 84
Bepple's Pies, 14
Betelnut, 13

Biking, 3, 25, 91
Biscuits 'n' Blues, 17
Blazing Saddles (bike shop), 25
Blue & Gold Fleet, 2, 24
Bottom of the Hill (bar), 79
Boulevard Restaurant, 66
Brasserie, 36

C

Cable Car Barn and Museum, 29
Cable cars, 59
Cadillac Bar, 79
Cafe Bastille, 68
Cafe de la Presse, 57
Cafe du Nord, 43
Caffe Trieste, 54
California Academy of Sciences, 87
California Culinary Academy, 36
California's Palace of the Legion of Honor, 90
Camping, 3
Campton Place Hotel Fashion Luncheons, 61
Careme Room, 36
Cartoon Art Museum, 71
Center for the Arts, 71
Chestnut Street shopping district, 14
China Beach, 84
Chinatown Adventures (tour), 55
Churches
  Glide Memorial Church, 38
  Grace Cathedral, 32
  Mission Dolores, 77
  Old Saint Mary's, 34
Circle Gallery, 56
City Art Tours, 55
City Lights Bookstore, 44
Cliff House Restaurant, 84
Clift Hotel's French Room, 57
Coconut Grove, 43
Coit Tower, 15, 42
Cruisin' the Castro (tour), 55
Cypress Club, 67

D

Day in Nature (tour), 69
DNA Lounge, 43

E

East Fort Baker, 15
Eddie Rickenbacker's, 79
El Toro, 76
Escape Artists Tours, 69
European Limousine Tours, 69
Exploratorium, 6

F

Fairmont Hotel, 33
Ferry rides, 2
Fillmore and Broadway (scenic vista), 52
Fillmore, the, 18
Finocchio's, 35
Flower Power Haight-Ashbury Tour, 55
Fort Mason Center, 10
Fragrance Garden, 91

G

Ghirardelli Chocolate Company, 22
Ghirardelli Square, 22
Glide Memorial Church, 38
Glorious Food Culinary Walking Tours, 55
Golden Gate Bridge, 85
Golden Gate Ferries, 2
Golden Gate Fortune Cookie Factory, 47
Golden Gate Golf Course, 89
Golden Gate Park, 91
Golfing, 89
Grace Cathedral, 32
Grant Avenue (walking tour), 63
Greens (restaurant), 10
Greenwich Steps (Hyde-Larkin), 31
Greenwich Steps (Hyde-Leavenworth), 31

H

Haight-Ashbury, 82
Haas-Lilienthal House, 11
Helen's Walk Tour, 55
Hi-Ball Lounge, 43
Horseback riding, 91
Hotel Boheme, 44
Hotels
  Archbishop's Mansion, 20
  Fairmont Hotel, 33
  Hotel Boheme, 44
  Hotel San Remo, 48
  Inn at the Opera, 39
  Radisson Miyako Hotel, 21
  Red Victorian Peace Center B & B, 83
  Sherman House, 12
  24 Henry, 80
  Villa Florence, 60
  Warwick Regis Hotel, 62
Hotel San Remo, 48
Hotel Utah (nightclub), 70
House of Nanking, 51
Hunting Bargains (tour), 69

I

Inn at the Opera (hotel), 39

J

Japan Center, 21
Japanese Moon-Viewing Garden, 91
Japanese Tea Garden, 88
Javawalk (tour), 55
Jewish Museum, 71

K

Kabuki Hot Springs, 21
Kayaking, 3
Kite flying, 8
Kuleto's Restaurant, 60

L

Larkin Steps, 31
Lawn bowling, 91
Lincoln Park Golf Course, 89
Lombard Street, 30
Lulu, 74

M

Malvina's Cafe, 50
Marina Green, 8
Marine World Africa USA, 98
Max's Opera Cafe, 40
M. H. de Young Memorial, 86
Mission Cliffs Indoor Climbing Center, 73
Mission Dolores, 77

Milieu (tour), 69
Monterey Bay Aquarium, 95
Monuments/sculptures
  Palace of Fine Arts, 9
  Philip Burton Statue, 10
  Wave Organ, 7
Morrison Planetarium, 87
Mount Tamalpais State Park, 15, 93
Muir Woods Redwood Park, 97
MUNI Bus No. 29, 5
Murals
  Coit Tower, 42
  Mission, 75
Murals of the Mission, 75
Museums
  Ansel Adams Center for
    Photography, 71
  Asian Art Museum, 86
  Bay Area Discovery Museum, 99
  Cable Car Barn and Museum, 29
  California Academy of Sciences,
    87
  California Palace of the Legion of
    Honor, 90
  Cartoon Art Museum, 71
  Center for the Arts, 71
  Circle Gallery, 56
  Exploratorium, 6
  Jewish Museum, 71
  M. H. de Young Memorial, 72
  Monterey Bay Aquarium, 95
  Morrison Planetarium, 87
  Presidio Museum, 4
  San Francisco Museum of Modern
    Art, 72
  San Francisco Natural History
    Museum, 87
  San Francisco Zoo, 92
  Steinhart Aquarium, 87

N

Napa Valley Wine Train, 94
New Orleans Room, 33, 35
Noontime concerts, Old Saint Mary's
  Cathedral, 34

O

Ocean Beach, 84
Octagon House, 11

Old Saint Mary's Cathedral, 34
Oliveto's (restaurant), 96

P

Pacific Heights, Mansions of, 16
Palace of Fine Arts, 9
Paradise Lounge, 70
Parks
  Alamo Square, 52
  Angel Island, 3
  Fort Mason Center, 10
  Fragrance Garden, 91
  Ghirardelli Square, 22
  Golden Gate Park, 91
  Japanese Moon-Viewing Garden, 91
  Japanese Tea Garden, 88
  Marina Green, 8
  Marine World Africa USA, 98
  Mount Tamalpais State Park, 93
  Muir Woods Redwood Park, 97
  Presidio, 4
  Rooftop Garden, Crocker Galleria,
    65
  Sea Lion Colony, 23
  Strybing Arboretum and Botanical
    Gardens, 91
  Sun Terrace, Zellerbach Building, 65
  Washington Square, 50
  Yerba Buena Gardens, 65
Pasta Pomodoro, 46
Philip Burton Statue, 10
Pier 39, 24
Pier 40 Roastery and Cafe, 57
Plush Room, 35
Presidio Museum, 4
Presidio, the, 4

R

Radisson Miyako Hotel, 21
Rasselas, 17
Red & White Fleet, 2
Red Victorian Peace Center B & B, 83
Repeat Performances (shop), 19
Restaurant at 2223 Market Street, 81
Restaurants
  Academy Grill, 36
  Act IV, 39
  Albona, 49
  Aqua, 64

Bay View Cafe, 23
Bepple's Pies, 14
Betelnut, 13
Biscuits 'n' Blues, 17
Boulevard Restaurant, 66
Brasserie, 36
Cafe Bastille, 68
Cafe de la Presse, 57
Caffé Trieste, 54
California Culinary Academy, 36
Campton Place Hotel Fashion
   Luncheons, 61
Careme Room, 36
Cliff House Restaurant, 84
Clift Hotel's French Room, 57
Cypress Club, 67
El Toro, 76
Greens, 10
House of Nanking, 51
Kuleto's Restaurant, 60
Lulu, 74
Malvina's Cafe, 50
Max's Opera Cafe, 40
Oliveto's, 96
Pasta Pomodoro, 46
Pier 40 Roastery and Cafe, 57
Restaurant at 2223 Market Street, 81
San Francisco Brewing Company, 41
Sherman House Dining Room, 12
Sinclair's Le Petit Cafe, 27
Slanted Door, 78
Swan's Oyster Depot, 28
Tonga Restaurant and Hurricane Bar,
   33
Vivande Ristorante, 37
Washington Square Bar and Grill, 50
Yoshi's Restaurant and Jazz Club, 101
Zax's, 53
Roller-blading, 91
Rooftop Garden, Crocker Galleria, 65
Rowing, 91
Running (race), 26

S

San Francisco Brewing Company, 41
San Francisco Museum of Modern Art,
   72
San Francisco Natural History
   Museum, 87
San Francisco Zoo, 92

Sausalito, 25
Scenic Bay Trail, 25
Scenic vistas and overlook points
   Alamo Square, 52
   Alcatraz, 1
   Cable cars, 59
   Coit Tower, 15, 42
   East Fort Baker, 15
   Fillmore and Broadway, 52
   Greenwich Steps (Hyde-Larkin), 31
   Greenwich Steps (Hyde-
     Leavenworth), 31
   Larkin Steps, 37
   Lombard Street, 30
   Mount Tamalpais, 15
   Twin Peaks, 15
   Vallejo Steps, 31
   Vallejo Street Garage (roof), 52
Sea Lion Colony, 23
Seconds to Go (shop), 19
Sherman House (hotel), 12
Shops and emporiums
   Bepple's Pies, 14
   Chestnut Street shopping district, 14
   Fillmore Street shopping district, 19
   Ghirardelli Chocolate Company, 22
   Ghirardelli Square, 22
   Pier 39, 24
   16th Street shopping district, 14
   Union Square, 56
   Union Street shopping district, 14
   Virgin Records Megastore, 58
Sinclair's Le Petit Cafe, 27
16th Street shopping district, 14
Slanted Door (restaurant), 78
Slim's, 70
Sports and recreation
   biking, 3, 25, 91
   camping, 3
   golfing, 89
   horseback riding, 91
   kayaking, 3
   kite flying, 8
   lawn bowling, 91
   roller-blading, 91
   rowing, 91
   running (race), 26
   swing dancing, 43
   tennis, 91
   wall-climbing, 73
Steinhart Aquarium, 87

Strybing Arboretum and Botanical
     Gardens, 91
Sun Terrace, Crown Zellerbach
     Garden, 65
Swan's Oyster Depot, 28
Swing dancing, 43

T

Tennis, 91
3 Babes and a Bus Nightclub Tours, 69
Tonga Restaurant and Hurricane Bar,
     33, 79
Tours, guided/organized
   Chinatown Adventures, 55
   City Art Tours, 55
   Cruisin' the Castro, 55
   Day in Nature, 69
   Escape Artists Tours, 69
   European Limousine Tours, 69
   ferry rides, 2
   Flower Power Haight-Ashbury Tour,
     55
   Glorious Food Culinary Walktours,
     55
   Golden Gate Park, 91
   Haas-Lilienthal House, 11
   Helen's Walk Tour, 55
   Hunting Bargains, 69
   Javawalk, 55
   Milieu, 69
   MUNI Bus No. 29, 5
   Napa Valley Wine Train, 94
   Octagon House, 11
   3 Babes and a Bus Nightclub Tours,
     69
Tours, self-guided
   Golden Gate Bridge, 85
   Golden Gate Fortune Cookie Factory,
     47
   Grant Avenue, 63
   Haight, the, 82
   Murals of the Mission, 75

Napa Valley, 100
Pacific Heights, mansions of, 16
Sausalito, 25
Scenic Bay Trail, 25
Sonoma Valley, 100
   wineries, Napa and Sonoma valleys,
     100
24 Henry (hotel), 80
Twin Peaks (scenic vista), 15

U

Union Square, 56
Union Street shopping district, 14
Up and Down Club, 70

V

Vallejo Steps, 31
Vallejo Street Garage (roof, scenic
     vista), 52
Victorian houses, 11
Villa Florence, 60
Virgin Records Megastore, 58
Vivande Ristorante, 37

W

Washington Square Bar and Grill, 50
Warwick Regis Hotel, 62
Wall-climbing, 73
Wave Organ, 7
Wineries, Napa and Sonoma
     valleys, 100

Y

Yerba Buena Gardens, 65, 71
Yoshi's Restaurant and Jazz Club, 101

Z

Zax's, 53